Universal Health Care

Other Books in the Current Controversies Series

Are There Two Americas?
The Confederate Flag
Deporting Immigrants
The Energy Industry
Enhanced Interrogation and Torture
Executive Orders
Freedom of Speech on Campus
Microaggressions, Safe Spaces, and Trigger Warnings
Police Training and Excessive Force
Political Extremism in the United States
States' Rights and the Role of the Federal Government

Universal Health Care

Kristina Lyn Heitkamp, Book Editor

GREENHAVEN
PUBLISHING

Published in 2019 by Greenhaven Publishing, LLC
353 3rd Avenue, Suite 255, New York, NY 10010

Copyright © 2019 by Greenhaven Publishing, LLC

First Edition

Articles in Greenhaven Publishing anthologies are often edited for length to meet page
requirements. In addition, original titles of these works are changed to clearly present
the main thesis and to explicitly indicate the author's opinion. Every effort is made to
ensure that Greenhaven Publishing accurately reflects the original intent of the authors.
Every effort has been made to trace the owners of the copyrighted material.

Cover image: Erik McGregor/PaciTc Press/LightRocket via Getty Images

Library of Congress Cataloging-in-Publication Data

Names: Heitkamp, Kristina Lyn, editor.
Title: Universal health care / Kristina Lyn Heitkamp, book editor.
Description: First edition. | New York : Greenhaven Publishing, 2019. |
  Series: Current controversies | Audience: Grade 9 to 12. | Includes
  bibliographical references and index.
Identifiers: LCCN 2018004959| ISBN 9781534503168 (library bound) | ISBN
  9781534503175 (paperback)
Subjects: LCSH: Medical policy—United States—Juvenile literature. | Health
  care reform—United States—Juvenile literature.
Classification: LCC RA395.A3 U586 2019 | DDC 362.10973—dc23
LC record available at https://lccn.loc.gov/2018004959

Manufactured in the United States of America

Website: http://greenhavenpublishing.com

Contents

Foreword   **11**

Introduction   **14**

Chapter 1: Should the United States Have Universal Health Care?

Health Care for All Is Plausible If the US Addresses   **18**
Inequalities

Richard Boudreau

The US health care system is in a terrible state of affairs. However, changing from a market-driven system to one that focuses on quality, access, and healthy lives could resuscitate the system.

Yes: Health Care Is a Human Right Recognized Around the World

Universal Health Care Coverage Is Inevitable   **25**

Ed Dolan

The American health care system is at the tipping point of disaster. Although several politicians resist the move to universal health care, the federal government already plays a big role in health care.

US Health Care Ranks Last Among Other Advanced   **30**
Economies

Jake Johnson

A study compares the failing US health care system with other advanced nations and finds that the US falls short in several areas, including access, equity, and efficiency.

Most Americans Want Universal Health Care, But   **33**
Politicians Are Cynical

Joshua Cho

Some Democrats are entirely in favor of affordable health care but think universal health care is a utopian idea. Pessimism regarding universal health care's implementation stands in its way.

No: Universal Health Care Would Break an Already Broken System

Universal Health Care Will Lead to Moral Hazard   **36**

Jose Almeida

A doctor reflects on the possibility of moral hazard with universal health care, which is the phenomenon of patients excessively visiting the doctor when they aren't responsible for the bill.

Government Health Care Means Less Innovation   **39**
and Lower Quality

Dennis Smith

Medicare is not a quality leader in health care, and there is evidence to prove it. Current enrollees in government-run health plans already have problems with access to quality care.

Chapter 2: Does the Cost of Universal Health Care Outweigh the Benefits?

US Spending, Services, Price, and Health Compared   **47**
to the Rest of the World

David Squires and Chloe Anderson

Compared to other high-income countries, the US spends far more. But despite the huge investment, the US ranks low on life expectancy and high in infant mortality.

Yes: Universal Health Care Would Bankrupt the US Government

"Medicare for All" Would Not Solve the Problem of   **57**
Rising Health Care Costs

David Hogberg

Proponents of shifting to a Medicare system say it would lower costs, but this analysis says that Medicare is part of the problem of suffering health care.

State Politicians Take the Lead in Providing   **65**
Universal Health Care

Pauline Bartolone

While the federal government fights over health care problems, the state of California proposes a state-run single-payer system.

Bernie Sanders's Single-Payer Health Care Plan Is a **69**
Total Disaster

Robert E. Moffit

Bernie Sanders proposed extending Medicare, but the plan would be costly and complicated.

No: Universal Health Care Would Be Economically Smart

The Case for Universal Health Care **73**

Kao-Ping Chua

The number of uninsured individuals in the US is increasing and health care quality is declining. There are costs associated with providing universal health care, but the economic return is priceless.

Medical Plutocrats Control the US Health Care System **81**

Robert Kuttner

Health care costs have risen while the quality of care has plummeted, and the medical insurance companies are to blame.

Learning from Diabetes: Why Smart Government **86**
Spending Matters

Niranjan Konduri

A global report on diabetes sheds light on how governments can ensure access to affordable and essential medicines and vaccines without having to spend an outrageous amount of money.

Chapter 3: Is the Government Responsible for Health Care?

Experts Debate Whether Health Care Is a Federal **91**
Responsibility

Julie Rovner

In this viewpoint, a professor of economics, a doctor, and other informed voices debate whether the government should provide universal health care for its citizens.

Yes: The US Government Can and Should Provide Health Care for Its Citizens

More Americans Say Government Should Ensure   **94**
Health Care Coverage

Kristen Bialik

As politicians battle it out over health care, a Pew Research Center survey reveals that more than half of Americans say the government should be responsible for health care coverage.

The French Health Care System: Low Costs, Great Care   **97**

Isabelle Durand-Zaleski

France has provided universal health care since 2000. This detailed primer explains how the French government manages to provide quality care to its citizens.

Universal Health Care Makes Everyone's Life Better   **106**

Kathleen A. Lavidge

After living in England for several years, Lavidge points out the big and small ways having access to health care positively affects the quality of life.

The Right to Health for Everyone   **110**

Office of the United Nations High Commissioner for Human Rights

Some groups of patients, such as children or migrants, face discrimination or socio-economic challenges in our current health system.

No: Health Care Is the Responsibility of Many, Not the Government

Accountable Care Organizations Help Health Care   **116**

Jenny Gold

Accountable care organizations are a step toward more effective health care without uprooting the entire system.

Doctors and Patients Take Matters into Their Own   **122**
Hands

Algorithms for Innovation

Determining who is responsible for US health care is complicated. But more doctors are collaborating in teams to take on this issue, while patients are being more proactive in their health choices.

US Health Care Is a Privilege, Not a Right   **129**

Agence France-Presse (AFP)

In the past, US health care has been viewed as a privilege for
the aging and poor population. Attempts at health care reform
have failed, while some Americans believe it's the individual's
responsibility.

Chapter 4: Will the Quality of Care Suffer with Universal Health Care?

Linking Health to Other Areas of Life   **133**

Sustainable Development Solutions Network (SDSN)

Health care and its relationship to other aspects of life reach far
and wide, impacting and being impacted by everything from
the economy and education to gender equality and sustainable
communities.

Yes: Care Would Get Worse, Not Better with Universal Health Care

Select Services with Universal Health Care   **139**

Peter C. Smith and Kalipso Chalkidou

In the debate surrounding universal health care, the question of
whether or not to establish a specific health benefit package is
considered. This viewpoint examines the pros and cons of a benefit
package.

Canada's Cautionary Tale of Universal Health Care   **148**

Candice Malcolm

A review of Canada's single-payer system shows that it falls short in
quality of care and is held up by its close neighbor: the US health care
industry.

No: The Quality of US Health Care Needs to Improve

Universal Health Coverage Contributes to Better Health   **153**

*Organisation for Economic Co-operation and Development
(OECD)*

A global report shows the many ways that universal health care has
a positive impact on health, including an increase in life expectancy
and financial risk protection.

The Republican War Against Universal Health Care   **157**

Kenneth Peres

From slashing funding for health programs and basic assistance to eliminating programs that help keep our environment healthy and safe, the Republican fight to eliminate the Affordable Health Care Act is taking down a lot more than expected.

Organizations to Contact   **168**

Bibliography   **171**

Index   **174**

Foreword

Controversy" is a word that has an undeniably unpleasant connotation. It carries a definite negative charge. Controversy can spoil family gatherings, spread a chill around classroom and campus discussion, inflame public discourse, open raw civic wounds, and lead to the ouster of public officials. We often feel that controversy is almost akin to bad manners, a rude and shocking eruption of that which must not be spoken or thought of in polite, tightly guarded society. To avoid controversy, to quell controversy, is often seen as a public good, a victory for etiquette, perhaps even a moral or ethical imperative.

Yet the studious, deliberate avoidance of controversy is also a whitewashing, a denial, a death threat to democracy. It is a false sterilizing and sanitizing and superficial ordering of the messy, ragged, chaotic, at times ugly processes by which a healthy democracy identifies and confronts challenges, engages in passionate debate about appropriate approaches and solutions, and arrives at something like a consensus and a broadly accepted and supported way forward. Controversy is the megaphone, the speaker's corner, the public square through which the citizenry finds and uses its voice. Controversy is the life's blood of our democracy and absolutely essential to the vibrant health of our society.

Our present age is certainly no stranger to controversy. We are consumed by fierce debates about technology, privacy, political correctness, poverty, violence, crime and policing, guns, immigration, civil and human rights, terrorism, militarism, environmental protection, and gender and racial equality. Loudly competing voices are raised every day, shouting opposing opinions, putting forth competing agendas, and summoning starkly different visions of a utopian or dystopian future. Often these voices attempt to shout the others down; there is precious little listening and considering among the cacophonous din. Yet listening and considering, too, are essential to the health of a democracy. If controversy is democracy's lusty lifeblood, respectful listening and careful thought are its higher faculties, its brain, its conscience.

Current Controversies does not shy away from or attempt to hush the loudly competing voices. It seeks to provide readers with as wide and representative as possible a range of articulate voices on any given controversy of the day, separates each one out to allow it to be heard clearly and fairly, and encourages careful listening to each of these well-crafted, thoughtfully expressed opinions, supplied by some of today's leading academics, thinkers, analysts, politicians, policy makers, economists, activists, change agents, and advocates. Only after listening to a wide range of opinions on an issue, evaluating the strengths and weaknesses of each argument, assessing how well the facts and available evidence mesh with the stated opinions and conclusions, and thoughtfully and critically examining one's own beliefs and conscience can the reader begin to arrive at his or her own conclusions and articulate his or her own stance on the spotlighted controversy.

This process is facilitated and supported in each Current Controversies volume by an introduction and chapter overviews that provide readers with the essential context they need to begin engaging with the spotlighted controversies, with the debates surrounding them, and with their own perhaps shifting or nascent opinions on them. Chapters are organized around several key questions that are answered with diverse opinions representing all points on the political spectrum. In its content, organization, and methodology, readers are encouraged to determine the authors' point of view and purpose, interrogate and analyze the various arguments and their rhetoric and structure, evaluate the arguments' strengths and weaknesses, test their claims against available facts and evidence, judge the validity of the reasoning, and bring into clearer, sharper focus the reader's own beliefs and conclusions and how they may differ from or align with those in the collection or those of classmates.

Research has shown that reading comprehension skills improve dramatically when students are provided with compelling, intriguing, and relevant "discussable" texts. The subject matter of these collections could not be more compelling, intriguing, or urgently relevant to today's students and the world they are poised to inherit. The anthologized articles also provide the basis for stimulating, lively, and passionate classroom debates. Students who are compelled to anticipate objections to their own argument and identify the flaws in those of an opponent read more carefully, think more critically, and steep themselves in relevant context, facts, and information more thoroughly. In short, using discussable text of the kind provided by every single volume in the Current Controversies series encourages close reading, facilitates reading comprehension, fosters research, strengthens critical thinking, and greatly enlivens and energizes classroom discussion and participation. The entire learning process is deepened, extended, and strengthened.

If we are to foster a knowledgeable, responsible, active, and engaged citizenry, we must provide readers with the intellectual, interpretive, and critical-thinking tools and experience necessary to make sense of the world around them and of the all-important debates and arguments that inform it. We must encourage them not to run away from or attempt to quell controversy but to embrace it in a responsible, conscientious, and thoughtful way, to sharpen and strengthen their own informed opinions by listening to and critically analyzing those of others. This series encourages respectful engagement with and analysis of current controversies and competing opinions and fosters a resulting increase in the strength and rigor of one's own opinions and stances. As such, it helps readers assume their rightful place in the public square and provides them with the skills necessary to uphold their awesome responsibility—guaranteeing the continued and future health of a vital, vibrant, and free democracy.

Introduction

> *"America's health care system is*
> *neither healthy, caring, nor a system."*
>
> > —*Walter Cronkite,*
> > *American journalist*

The American health care system is broken. According the United States Census Bureau's 2016 report, 28.1 million Americans are still without health insurance coverage. Administrative costs, such as faxing health records or making phone calls to verify patient insurance coverage, eat up over $300 billion annually.[1] Medical errors are the third leading cause of death in the country.[2] Mistakes range from diagnostic errors, to communication breakdowns, to mix-ups with medication doses. Despite all the money siphoned into health care and the country's lead in medical innovation, the quality of the US health care system ranks brutally low compared to other developed nations.

Defining what American health care involves is a convoluted and confusing process. The United States does not have a single nationwide system of care. There are many players in the system, including private health insurance provided through employers or public insurance programs like Medicare or Medicaid. When someone visits a clinic or hospital to receive goods and services—like an x-ray or prescription—the bill is paid either by a private or public insurance provider or by the uninsured patient. Because the system is disjointed and dispersed, it is not very efficient or effective.

Americans often gripe about the state of our health care system and its massive defects, but what is the resolution? Looking at examples that work around the world, some wonder if universal health care is the best solution to our flawed system.

Universal health care is a single-payer health care system in which the government—not a private insurer—pays for health care. Health care services may still be provided by private practices, but they are paid for by the government. The funds used to pay for health care services, such as doctor wages, medical devices, or drugs, come from taxes. Universal health care strives to provide quality care with equity in access without the risk of financial hardship. A study published in the *American Journal of Medicine* reports that the number one reason for bankruptcy is medical debt. Universal health care means that regardless of economic status, a patient is guaranteed access to prevention, treatment, and rehabilitation care.

Sounds good, right? But even though universal health care seems like an ideal solution in theory, there is much controversy and debate surrounding whether or not it's up to the job.

Proponents of universal health care say that health care is a basic human right recognized all over the world, that it is not simply a privilege. They argue that a single-payer system would allow lives to be saved, health care costs to decrease, and economic productivity to prosper. Dr. Margaret R. McLean, Associate Director of Bioethics at the Markkula Center for Applied Ethics of Santa Clara University, explains why it's the government's duty to provide care for its citizens in her article titled "Expanding Health Care Coverage: A Balm for California?"

> The inherent dignity of human persons requires that people be treated with dignity and respect, which includes the fulfillment of the basic human need for health care … Health is a fundamental good necessary for human flourishing and health care is a fundamental human right. Because health care, at its best, promotes and sustains human health, society is obligated to provide access to basic quality health care for all its members.

However, those who oppose universal health care believe that handing over an already broken system to the government is not the answer to our health care problems. Opponents argue that a single-payer government-run system would increase the US debt and deficit. Taxes would go up, and the quality of health care might suffer as well. They argue that citizens need to take ownership for their own health, that health care is a not a handout. American physician and politician Rand Paul voiced his opinion of what a right to health care implies:

> If I'm a physician in your community and you say you have a right to health care, do you have a right to beat down my door with the police, escort me away and force me to take care of you? That's ultimately what the right to free health care would be. If you believe in a right to health care, you're believing in basically the use of force to conscript someone to do your bidding.[3]

Health care affects everyone, and many voices are involved in the debate. These include health care providers who are on the frontline, serving the public and asking important questions about the shared responsibility of care, along with business owners who believe universal health care is not the silver-bullet answer to rising health care costs. The viewpoints in *Current Controversies: Universal Health Care* explore the complexity of the debate and offer a platform for readers to navigate and vote in the interest of their best health care option.

Notes

1. Wikler E, Basch P, Cutler D: "Paper Cuts—Reducing Health Care Administrative Costs." Washington, DC: Center for American Progress; 2012.

2. Makary Martin A, Daniel Michael. "Medical error—the third leading cause of death in the US," BMJ 2016; 353 :i2139.

3. United States Senate Health, Education, Labor and Pensions subcommittee hearing, "Diverting Non-Urgent Emergency Room Use: Can It Provide Better Care and Lower Costs?" help.senate.gov, May 11, 2011.

CHAPTER 1

Should the United States Have Universal Health Care?

Health Care for All Is Plausible If the US Addresses Inequalities

Richard Boudreau

Dr. Richard Boudreau is a maxillo-facial surgeon, attorney at law, forensic expert, and bioethicist who attended the University of Southern California, Harvard University, University of California Irvine, the University of Washington, the University of Hamburg, Loyola Marymount University, Pepperdine University, and the University of Oxford.

Though the United States is one of the wealthiest nations in the world, the disparities in income are only surpassed by the inequalities in access to health care. Because of the close tie between the health care crisis and the fiscal health of the country as a whole, proposals have been made to introduce universal health care, to adapt existing systems and to support efforts, including what has been deemed "ObamaCare" to move towards greater accountability in obtaining and maintaining health insurance for the millions of uninsured and underinsured. Though most countries in the developed world perceive health care as a basic human right, the United States has yet to determine a way of creating and funding a single-payer universal health care system that will address the inequalities that exist and provide a better option for preventative medicine, interventive medicine, and long-term care.

One of the central problems for this country is that our political process is divided ideologically and health care paradigms do not appear to address issues on both sides. While there is support for a national health program that would ensure access to the working poor, fiscal conservatives view this as a system that cannot be afforded and that would expand debt in an uncontrollable

"The Plausibility of Universal Health Care in the United States," by Richard Boudreau, Clin Res Bioeth, February 4, 2017. https://www.omicsonline.org/open-access/the-plausibility-of-universal-health-care-in-the-united-states-2155-9627-1000298 .php?aid=87185. Licensed under CC BY 4.0.

manner. In fact, there is a clear division between the patriarchal perspectives of the democrats and the growing Tea Party call for personal responsibility.

The following study considers the issue of health care in this country, including the current level of expenditure, the lack of access, comparable international efforts, and even state proposed changes that have shown some success in the implementation of universal health care. This study will focus on the way in which innovation and governance have struggled to determine workable paradigms for health care reform. The focus on a single-payer or universal health care system has not led to successful legislative change, and so elements of both arguments will be considered when addressing the best methods for improving access to care and affordability. A proposed plan will be introduced that will consider the best options for improving the following: 1. Affordability; 2. Access to care; 3. Long-term viability; 4. State and federal cooperation; 5. Distribution of funding or services. The proposed plan will address these issues and present some plausible approaches.

United States and Health Care

Though the United States is one of the world's wealthiest nations, the current economic downturn has served to emphasize the gap between the wealthy and the average Americans. One of the strongest indicators of wealth in this country has become access to health care. While the wealthy are able to afford every luxurious health care service, from private rooms to elective surgeries, the average American cannot afford a basic level of preventative care.

The Industry

Health care is a multi-trillion dollar industry in the United States and includes providers, insurers and government regulators that dictate the pricing and processes involved in the allocation of health care resources. The following statistics reflect some of the challenges and issues with the health care industry in this country, especially in reference to the allocation of resources:

- In 2005, the US spent $2 trillion on health care, which is 16 percent of GDP and $6,697 per person.
- Health care costs have grown on average 2.5 percentage points faster than US gross domestic product since 1970.
- Almost half of health care spending is used to treat just 5 percent of the population.
- Prescription drug spending is 10 percent of total health spending but contributes to 14 percent of the growth in spending.
- While about 26 percent of the poor spent more than 10 percent of their income on health in 1996, the number increased to 33 percent by 2003.
- Many policy experts believe new technologies and the spread of existing ones account for a large portion of medical spending and its growth [1].

The current economic downturn and high unemployment rates have led to an even larger portion of the population falling into the category of the uninsured or underinsured, with a large portion of the working poor being unable to meet their basic health care needs.

While health care takes up a large slice of the economic "pie" in this country, it seems surprising that so many Americans go without essential services [1]. Health care costs are becoming an increasing problem, especially for low-income families. These families are spending an increasing share of their income on health care essentials, making health care the faster growing segment of the national economy consuming a large percentage of the average family's yearly income. In 1970, for example, health care costs were about $356 per year on average. In 40 years, that amount grew to about $6,697 per person, making the health care industry one of the leading industries in this country, taking in approximately $2 trillion annually [1]. Current projections indicate that health care spending will consume approximately more than 1/5 of the gross domestic product of this country by 2016 [1].

Bartlett and Steele [2] maintain that the American health care system is in critical condition, primarily the result of the creation of a market-driven system for medical care and the increasing competition between health insurers driving costs upward. The creation of a health care system that is market driven creates a situation that is often oppositional: the process of providing services is costly, while the directive for market-driven companies is to make money. This viewpoint has been supported in major national movements towards implementing a national health system and in criticisms that maintain that the United States, though a country with one of the largest health care infrastructures, scores relatively low in terms of health care access and health outcomes for the masses.

Some believe that the issues with the American health care system relate to changes that occurred in the 1980s during the Reagan Administration [2]. Prior to that time, the health care system was based primarily in the existence of non-profit hospitals and health care facilities with a focus on providing services for illness prevention, emergent care and long-term care. Reorganization of the nation's hospitals under a free-market directive led to the creation of massive moneymaking health care conglomerates, uniting providers, facilities and insurance companies in an organizational structure directed towards profit. Because health services cost money and corporate health organizations are seeking to make money, patient care has suffered significantly as these companies have grown more powerful [2].

One of the central problems with allowing for a market-driven health care system is that there are fewer providers, hospitals and health care facilities than there is need. As a result, the cost of health care in the United States has skyrocketed. Rather than improving the product (health care) or improving the delivery system, the free market enterprise of health care has translated into a decline in health care conditions (because they can) and an increase in cost. Not only has this translated into poor health care in many urban centers, but it has also created a system that makes illness prevention cost-prohibitive to the underinsured or uninsured.

Bartlett and Steele [2] maintain that the government has turned the issue over to the private organizations and asked them to sort out the profit-driven process through which health care has developed. As an increasing number of health care organizations and hospitals nationwide have become moneymaking devices, the number of people served and the level of care decline. In these corporate monstrosities, health care is both a service and a commodity and so health care organizations have rejected a consumer focus and defined a focus on profit. Rather than creating a level of competitiveness, as suggested in the Reagan Administration's call for a focus on market-driven health care, the health care system is driven by such a great profit motive that it becomes easy to reject a compassionate response to the care needs of the many and seek out ways of providing care for those who can pay the most for it.

[...]

The following are the major findings of a comparative study of the United States and other developed nations:

- Quality: The indicators of quality were grouped into four categories: right (or effective) care, safe care, coordinated care, and patient-centered care. Compared with the other five countries, the US fares best on provision and receipt of preventive care, a dimension of "right care." However, its low scores on chronic care management and safe, coordinated, and patient-centered care pull its overall quality score down. Other countries are further along than the US in using information technology and a team approach to manage chronic conditions and coordinate care. Information systems in countries like Germany, New Zealand, and the UK enhance the ability of physicians to identify and monitor patients with chronic conditions. Such systems also make it easy for physicians to print out medication lists, including those prescribed by other physicians. Nurses help patients manage their chronic diseases, with those services financed by governmental programs.

- Access: Not surprising—given the absence of universal coverage—people in the US go without needed health care because of cost more often than people do in the other countries. Americans were the most likely to say they had access problems related to cost, but if insured, patients in the US have rapid access to specialized health care services. In other countries, like the UK and Canada, patients have little to no financial burden but experience long wait times for such specialized services. The US and Canada rank lowest on the prompt accessibility of appointments with physicians, with patients more likely to report waiting six or more days for an appointment when needing care. Germany scores well on patients' perceptions of access to care on nights and weekends and on the ability of primary care practices to make arrangements for patients to receive care when the office is closed. Overall, Germany ranks first on access.

- Efficiency: On indicators of efficiency, the US ranks last among the six countries, with the UK and New Zealand ranking first and second, respectively. The US has poor performance on measures of national health expenditures and administrative costs as well as on measures of the use of information technology and multidisciplinary teams. Also, of sicker respondents who visited the emergency room, those in Germany and New Zealand are less likely to have done so for a condition that could have been treated by a regular doctor, had one been available.

- Equity: The US ranks a clear last on all measures of equity. Americans with below-average incomes were much more likely than their counterparts in other countries to report not visiting a physician when sick, not getting a recommended test, treatment or follow-up care, not filling a prescription, or not seeing a dentist when needed because of costs. On each of these indicators, more than two-fifths of lower-income adults in the US said they went without needed care because of costs in the past year.

- Healthy lives: The US ranks last overall with poor scores on all three indicators of healthy lives. The US and UK had much higher death rates in 1998 from conditions amenable to medical care—with rates 25 to 50 percent higher than Canada and Australia. Overall, Australia ranks highest on healthy lives, scoring first or second on all of the indicators [3].

The findings underscore the need to address some of the essential problems in this country related to providing health care in a manner that allows for equity in access and improves outcomes.

[...]

References

Kaiser Family Foundation (2007) Key information on health care costs and their impact.

Bartlett D, Steele J (2004) Critical Condition: How Health Care in America Became Big Business and Bad Medicine. DoubleDay, New York.

Davis K, Schoen C, Schoenbaum S, Doty M, Holmgren A (2007) Mirror, mirror on the wall: An international update on the comparative performance of American health care.

Universal Health Care Coverage Is Inevitable

Ed Dolan

Edwin G. Dolan holds a PhD in economics from Yale University. He has taught at Dartmouth College, the University of Chicago, George Mason University, and Gettysburg College. He is currently a senior fellow at the Niskanen Center and lives in Northwest Michigan.

Many observers are describing the dramatic failure of the American Health Care Act (AHCA) as a debacle, but perhaps it will prove to be a step forward. As everyone knows by now, the United States is alone among advanced economies in not having universal access to healthcare, but it is already much closer to such a system than most people realize. The defeat of the AHCA may be a tipping point in which the forces trying to figure out how to make universal access health care work gain the upper hand over those that are fighting it.

The True Scope of Government in Our Healthcare System

The term "single payer" is often used to describe the healthcare systems of other high-income countries. Although that is a convenient term, it is not entirely accurate. As the following chart of healthcare spending in OECD countries shows, all countries use a mix of private and public payments. Furthermore, even in many countries where the government share of spending is high, the actual administration of payments is split among several funds, trusts, or regional agencies. There are no countries where all health-related services, including optical and dental services, drugs, and long-term care, are entirely free to patients without co-pays or deductibles. Healthcare systems of OECD countries also

"Universal Healthcare Access Is Coming. Stop Fighting It and Start Figuring Out How to Make It Work," by Ed Dolan, Niskanen Center, March 28, 2017. Reprinted by permission.

differ widely in such aspects as whether facilities are publically or privately owned, whether doctors are public employees or independent practitioners, and whether private provision of healthcare, in competition with public services, is encouraged or discouraged.

In the United States, as elsewhere, even the public healthcare sector is not a true single-payer system. The federal government already operates three large systems: Medicare, Medicaid, and the Veterans Administration. Each of the first two is comparable in size to the entire healthcare systems of most European countries. If we categorize healthcare expenditures by the type of primary payer, the three big federal programs accounted for roughly a third of all spending in 2015, according to data from the Centers for Medicare and Medicaid Services.

However, this perspective understates the extent of the government role in US healthcare. If we categorize expenditures by the source of the funds (instead of the type of payer) the government share of spending is much larger. This is partly because state and local governments account for 17 percent of all healthcare spending. According to data from the Tax Policy Center, deductions and exclusions of health insurance premiums and related tax breaks cost the federal government some $250 billion in revenue in 2015—a substantial burden on the federal budget.

Deductibility of employer healthcare expenditures accounts for about three-fifths of total tax expenditures. Others include exclusions of Medicaid benefits from declared income, deductibility of insurance for self-employed individuals, tax breaks for some types of out-of-pocket costs, and other items. If we categorize healthcare expenditures according to the ultimate source of funds rather than the primary payer, we find that government budgets account for over half of all spending.

Our Faltering Private Insurance System

Both the Affordable Care Act (ACA or "Obamacare") and the AHCA tried to salvage what is left of private healthcare finance.

Yet its two pillars, employer-sponsored insurance and individual insurance plans, are beyond saving.

The individual insurance market is failing because too large a share of health care risks is inherently uninsurable. Two conditions must hold for a real insurance market to work. First, the risks in question must be *fortuitous*—that is, predictable statistically but not predictable for any particular individual. Second, premiums must be high enough to cover claims and administrative expenses, yet still be affordable to the customer.

Neither condition holds for individual health insurance. The principal reason is that a tiny share of the population accounts for the great bulk of all healthcare spending. Based on data from the Kaiser Family Foundation, the top 10 percent of households account for two-thirds of all personal healthcare spending and the top 5 percent for half of all spending. The majority of these high spenders have one or more chronic conditions that keep their spending high year after year.

The skewed pattern of spending poses a dilemma for policymakers: If they allow insurance companies to refuse to issue policies to people with pre-existing conditions, the people most in need of medical care will not be able to buy policies. If they insist on guaranteed issue, then the presence of high spenders in the risk pool pushes up premiums for everyone. As that happens, relatively healthy people drop out of the pool, pushing claims and premiums higher still for those who remain. As losses mount, insurers begin to drop out, too, until the system collapses.

Both the ACA and the AHCA opted for guaranteed issue. That sounds good politically, since many of us know a neighbor or relative with a pre-existing condition even if we don't have one ourselves. Ultimately, though, guaranteed issue is an unsustainable policy that threatens the whole individual insurance market with a "death spiral." The ACA is already showing early signs of such a spiral, and, as I explained in this earlier post, the AHCA seemed designed to make things worse rather than better.

Meanwhile, employer-sponsored health insurance has problems of its own. First, it works much better for large corporations than for small businesses. Most small firms simply do not have enough employees to constitute an affordably insurable risk pool. Second, economists believe that over time, employees end up bearing the cost of healthcare benefits through lower pay. Rising employer healthcare costs are thus a major contributor to the stagnation of wages. Third, the fear of losing insurance coverage makes people reluctant to give up jobs that are otherwise unsuitable—reluctant to try something new or start a business of their own. This "job lock," in turn, reduces labor mobility and makes the economy less able to respond to shocks from new technologies and changing patterns of trade.

For these reasons, job-linked health insurance has been gradually dying for some time now. According to another report from the Kaiser Family Foundation, from 1999 to 2014, the share of the nonelderly population covered by employer-sponsored insurance fell from 67 percent to 56 percent. If the AHCA had passed, its repeal of the ACA's employer mandate would have locked in the downward trend. The Congressional Budget Office estimated that over ten years, 7 million employees would have lost employer-sponsored insurance as a result of the AHCA.

What Lies Ahead

Despite the best of intentions, the ACA has been unable to save private-sector health insurance in either its individual or employer-sponsored form. The AHCA, the only alternative Republicans could offer, would only have accelerated the decline. That leaves two possibilities. Either the share of the population without effective access to the healthcare system will begin to rise again, or the government share of the national healthcare budget will continue to grow.

Decreased access may be the outcome in the short run. Republicans may make another attempt at reform that saves money through reduced coverage, but even if they abandon that legislative path and leave the ACA as the law of the land, its prospects are not good. Even with the greatest administrative energy behind it, it would be hard to make the ACA's private insurance market work well, and it is more likely that current administrators will work to undermine than to support its operation.

In the long run, however, collapse of the ACA is unlikely to prove politically acceptable, once it actually starts to hit home. Looking at CBO projection of decreased coverage is one thing; waking up in the morning to find that Aunt Sally can't get her chemo or Uncle John can't get his bypass surgery is another thing altogether. At that point, some form of universal healthcare access, whether we call it single payer or something else, will be the only option left.

And really, it is not such a bad alternative. A revealing report from the Commonwealth Fund ranks US healthcare eleventh out of eleven against those of ten high-income countries, all with systems that offer universal access. US healthcare is at the top in terms of cost and at the bottom in terms of efficiency and equity. And no, contrary to the scare stories, other countries do not use death panels or endless waiting periods to ration care. The United States ranks in the middle of the pack on measures of timeliness of care, although it is the worst of the eleven in terms of cost-related limitations on access.

So get used to it. We, too, could free up a good chunk of our national income now spent on healthcare, reduce medical insecurity, and cut the high administrative costs of our fragmented and overlapping healthcare systems. Universal healthcare access is coming. Stop fighting it and start figuring out how to make it work here, as it does elsewhere.

US Health Care Ranks Last Among Other Advanced Economies

Jake Johnson

Jake Johnson is a staff writer for Common Dreams.

N o, in turns out, the United States does not have the "best healthcare system in the world."

In the midst of a deeply unpopular attempt by the Republican Party to pass legislation that could leave 22 million more Americans uninsured and as support for Medicare for All soars, a new analysis published on Friday by the Washington-based Commonwealth Fund finds that the US healthcare system currently ranks last among 11 other advanced countries in healthcare outcomes, access, equity, and efficiency.

The US "fell short" in almost every domain measured, the Commonwealth Fund's senior vice president for policy and research Eric Schneider, M.D., told the *New Scientist*.

The study examines the healthcare systems of the US, the United Kingdom, France, Sweden, and several other nations, utilizing surveys of physicians and patients as well as data accumulated by the World Health Organization (WHO) and the Organization for Economic Cooperation and Development (OECD).

The report's conclusion echoes those of previous studies, which have indicated that despite spending far more on healthcare than other advanced nations, the US continues to lag behind in a variety of measures, from infant mortality rate to overall life expectancy.

Schneider and his co-authors—Dana Sarnak, David Squires, Arnav Shah, and Michelle Doty—observed that "[t]he US healthcare system is unique in several respects. Most striking: it is the only

high-income country lacking universal health insurance coverage."
The researchers went on to summarize their findings:

> The United States spends far more on healthcare than other high-income countries, with spending levels that rose continuously over the past three decades. Yet the US population has poorer health than other countries. Life expectancy, after improving for several decades, worsened in recent years for some populations, aggravated by the opioid crisis. In addition, as the baby boom population ages, more people in the US—and all over the world—are living with age-related disabilities and chronic disease, placing pressure on health care systems to respond.
>
> Timely and accessible healthcare could mitigate many of these challenges, but the US health care system falls short, failing to deliver indicated services reliably to all who could benefit.

As opposed to nations that guarantee healthcare to all, the authors concluded that Americans' ability to attain quality healthcare is almost entirely dependent on financial status.

"Your level of income defines the healthcare you receive far more in the United States than in other wealthy nations," the authors note.

While acknowledging that the Affordable Care Act (aka Obamacare) had much success in providing coverage to low-income Americans—particularly through the law's expansion of Medicaid—Commonwealth Fund President David Blumenthal, M.D., said the US healthcare system is "still not working as well as it could for Americans, and it works especially poorly for those with middle or lower incomes."

Underscoring this point, the Commonwealth Fund's analysis noted that "in the US, 44 percent of lower income and 26 percent of higher income people reported financial barriers to care." In the UK, these percentages are seven and four.

"A higher-earning person in the US is more likely to meet cost barriers than a low-income person in the UK," Schneider observed.

The survey comes as the Senate GOP is currently scrambling to convince enough Republicans to vote for a bill that, if enacted, would drastically cut Medicaid, defund Planned Parenthood, and potentially cause the deaths of thousands.

Blumenthal concludes that while there are substantial and urgent problems with the healthcare status quo, the Republicans' legislative efforts would "certainly exacerbate these challenges as millions would lose access to health insurance and affordable healthcare."

Most Americans Want Universal Health Care, But Politicians Are Cynical

Joshua Cho

Joshua Cho is a recent graduate of Boston College, an aspiring journalist, and a former intern at Fairness & Accuracy in Reporting.

After strong opposition from Americans concerned with the potential repeal of the Affordable Care Act and opposition from Senate Republicans forced Mitch McConnell to delay the Senate vote on the American Health Care Act, and growing support across the country for a single-payer health care system, the time is ripe for a push towards truly universal health care.

Despite the opportunities afforded amidst the current situation and the Trump administration's plummeting approval ratings, as well as more than half of House Democrats co-sponsoring Rep. John Conyer's (MI) single-payer bill, many high-profile Democrats continue to employ cynical rhetoric in their subtle refusal to endorse a truly universal health care system.

Instead, Americans are forced to witness the opportunistic spectacle of Democrats like Sen. Cory Booker (NJ) professing their belief that health care is a right and not a privilege; the same Cory Booker who was one of 13 Democrats to vote against legislation allowing Americans to import cheaper Canadian prescription drugs, while simultaneously refusing to endorse either a single-payer or national health service system.

Other cynical uses of political rhetoric can be seen in statements made by high-profile Democrats like Rep. John Lewis (GA) who argue that "Affordable health care is the birthright of every American," despite dismissing universal health care because "there's not anything free in America." The carefully added qualifier "affordable" is the operative word that betrays their true belief that health care isn't actually a right, but a commodity to be sold on the market, rationed out by consumers' ability to pay. And there are always going to be people priced out of markets.

People are correct to be outraged that the American Health Care Act is estimated to cause an additional 22 million people to be uninsured by 2026, but under the Affordable Care Act right now, there are 28 million people who are priced out of health insurance markets and remain uninsured. In a country where the majority of Americans don't have enough savings to cover a $500 emergency, it's no surprise that even the insured can face immense medical debt, with medical expenses being the No. 1 reason Americans file for personal bankruptcy.

Notwithstanding the shortcomings of the Affordable Care Act, former president Barack Obama claimed that progressives who backed Sen. Bernie Sanders' (VT) presidential campaign and Medicare-for-All proposal undermined the popularity of the program and contributed to its vulnerability. The irony of Obama's later challenge in his farewell address and claim to support a program that would insure more people at lower costs than the Affordable Care Act was palpable: "If anyone can put together a plan that is demonstrably better than the improvements we've made to our health care system—that covers as many people at less cost—I will publicly support it."

Obama's challenge has already been met by almost every other industrialized country, where universal health care plans like single-payer and national health service systems cover everyone at far lower costs than our current privatized system.

Yet, high-profile Democrats like Debbie Wasserman-Schultz continue to stonewall on support for a single-payer system and argue for the flaccid strategy of working within the Affordable Care Act because single-payer isn't politically viable: "If politically, Medicare-for-All actually became viable, if we elected enough people to Congress, that could make it happen, then I most definitely would be supportive of it."

Wasserman-Schultz's tepid response to a question on her support for single-payer is a reflection of compelling arguments made by political-philosophers like Michael Sandel in *What Money Can't Buy*, on how markets crowd out morals in public discourse and why we forbid markets in organ transplants—because the buying and selling of goods like human organs degrades them by inappropriately valuing them in terms of monetary worth.

If many of us already recognize the moral hideousness of trafficking in human organs because that would prioritize and value wealthier patients over poorer patients and those who need them the most, why should we permit trafficking in health insurance where private health insurers have perverse incentives to refuse coverage to those who need it the most and have similar outcomes to markets in human organs?

As some have already noted, Democrats who oppose the American Health Care Act without also supporting single-payer agree in principle that Americans should be allowed to die for the sake of rapacious private health insurers' profits and are just haggling over numbers.

Health care is a fundamental human right that should be accessible to anyone regardless of his or her ability to pay for it, which is also outlined in the UN's Universal Declaration of Human Rights; and if we correctly wouldn't stand it if we heard Democrats say that they refuse to stand up for the civil rights of minorities because it isn't "politically viable," why should we allow our elected officials to make excuses for not fighting for our right to health care until it becomes "politically viable," instead of right now?

And when we keep in mind that America's health care crisis is currently causing many to rely on crowdfunding platforms like GoFundMe and YouCaring for medical expenses, "cynical" is the appropriate word to describe Democrats who claim to support health care as a right, while simultaneously refusing to make health care anything but an "affordable" commodity.

Universal Health Care Will Lead to Moral Hazard

Jose Almeida

Jose Almeida is the founder and Medical Director of the Miami Vein Center. He is the creator and course director of the International Vein Congress (IVC), the largest educational summit dedicated to venous disease, which is now in its second decade.

With the Affordable Care Act (ACA) enrollment period coming to a close, we have an opportunity to reflect upon present challenges in our healthcare system and look to make improvements in the New Year.

And there is much to improve upon. There are rising premiums sweeping the nation, particularly in Arizona, Alabama and Nebraska. The medical community has been confronted with a huge increase in regulations, slowing down doctors and staff while doing little to actually improve patient care.

Healthcare plans have become increasingly comprehensive, now covering a breadth of services ranging from obesity counseling to the morning-after pill. While some of these offerings can improve a patient's health and quality of life, they present the problem of the moral hazard, a term describing how people behave when they are insured against losses.

In terms of healthcare, this has translated to people using their medical services and going to the doctor more often than necessary because they are not footing the cost. Unfortunately, the moral hazard has also inadvertently led to doctors themselves cashing in on the system, favoring volume over value and offering patients unnecessary treatments and procedures for their own financial gain.

"Challenging the moral hazard with healthcare and insurance," by Jose Almeida, The Hill, December 28, 2016. Reprinted by Permission. First published in The Hill, at: http://thehill.com/blogs/pundits-blog/healthcare/312035-challenging-the-moral-hazard-in-healthcare-and-insurance.

I see it constantly. Healthy patients come in to visit me who have had spider veins treated with laser ablation, a process that essentially collapses the veins. On the surface, it sounds innocuous—doctors promising their patients that they can get rid of unsightly veins with a quick and painless procedure. But the problem is that this treatment rarely eliminates the unsightly veins that "required" it in the first place. Furthermore, it destroys the veins that are most commonly used for heart bypass surgeries, potentially robbing patients of a lifesaving procedure they may need down the road.

While laser ablation is at times medically necessary for those who suffer from varicose veins that weaken their legs or cause pain, it should not be used to achieve cosmetic results. Unfortunately for patients, it's a real moneymaker, and the moral hazard is to blame.

Technology has led to some amazing advancements in the medical world: we are able to successfully treat cancer; vaccinate against a host of diseases; and life expectancy has risen to unprecedented levels. On the flip side, technology has also made some procedures so simple that any doctor can learn them. While on the surface this may sound like a positive, there is also a dark side. With laser ablation, for example, a family practitioner can take a weekend course on the procedure and call himself a vein doctor on Monday morning.

Doctors with distressingly low levels of training are able to open up their own vein clinics, pushing medically unnecessary procedures like laser ablation on patients who could get those results with a pair of compression stockings from Walgreens.

For a quick 30-minute laser ablation treatment, doctors can make as much as $2,000. They do this by working the system, embellishing records to suggest that a procedure is medically necessary in order to justify insurance coverage. This, of course, is all happening at the expense of the patient, and the consequent conflict of interest has completely disrupted the doctor/patient relationship.

There has been a 6,000 percent increase in laser ablation treatments within the last 10 years. In my home state of Florida, unnecessary laser ablations have risen to abnormally high levels.

The figures are staggering, and The Centers for Medicare & Medicaid Services (CMS) has never seen anything like it.

How do we fix this problem? Catastrophic events should undoubtedly be covered by insurance, but perhaps we need to move towards a value-based system, one in which doctors are not incentivized for pushing unnecessary treatments. In doing so, we can all work towards repairing the doctor/patient relationship while addressing abuse within the system.

Government Health Care Means Less Innovation and Lower Quality

Dennis Smith

Dennis Smith is a former senior fellow for the Center for Health Policy Studies at the Heritage Foundation.

[...]

Professor Jacob S. Hacker, professor of political science at the University of California at Berkeley and the leading proponent of a new government-run health plan, believes that the current system is "enormously wasteful, ill-targeted, inefficient, and unfair."[1] Beyond that, says Hacker, America's "health financing system is an economic and moral disaster."[2]

While these kinds of shrill attacks have become more commonplace in recent years among liberal policy analysts, they are routinely combined with false promises of a superior system of care run directly by government officials. But these ideological promises have little basis in fact. Indeed, congressional rhetoric notwithstanding, health care quality would play a minor role in the new schematic, especially in light of the proponents' reliance on traditional Medicare to deliver high-quality health care. In reality, Medicare, which has enormous gaps in coverage and is persistently plagued by congressionally engineered inefficiencies, provides no such thing.

The Politics of Government-Controlled Health Care

By creating a new government-run health plan, its proponents would achieve the same political objective as would a single-payer system—and it would be able to do so without stirring the traditional fears that accompany the expansion of government control. Writing in October 2006, Professor Hacker observes:

"The Real Price of a Public Health Plan: Less Innovation and Lower Quality," by Dennis Smith, The Heritage Foundation, April 24, 2009. Reprinted by permission.

There's much to be said for a single-payer system. Countries that have taken this route spend much less to provide secure insurance to everyone than the United States does to provide incomplete and insecure coverage to less than 85 percent of the population. Yet these advantages—guaranteed coverage and effective cost control—could be achieved without going all the way to a single national program, with all the public skepticism and political opposition that such a program would surely engender. Yes, Americans like Medicare and yes, Medicare is easy to explain. But that doesn't mean most people are ready to say everyone should be covered by Medicare. Many of us remain stubbornly attached to employment-based health insurance, and proposing to abolish it entirely is likely to stir up fear as well as gratitude.[3]

Bypassing Regular Order

Professor Hacker wrote that the "greatest lesson of the failure of comprehensive health reform in the past is that politics comes first. If real estate is about location, location, location, health reform is about politics, politics, politics."[4] Hacker further advised that the "core elements of reform need to be put in the budget, where they are free of the threat of a Senate filibuster (which requires 60 votes to overcome), and organized pressure will need to be put on Republicans and wavering Democrats to ensure they do the right thing."[5] In summary, says Professor Hacker, such is "the kind of bargain that could give compromise a good name—if the left would pursue it."[6]

It appears that with the strong support of the congressional leadership in the House of Representatives, at least, the Left is indeed prepared to pursue such a strategy, bypass regular order for consideration of health care reform, and attempt to enact a major overhaul of the American health care system without a bipartisan consensus.

[...]

Measuring Gaps in Quality

Much of Professor Hacker's proposal focuses on *why* health care would be more efficient under the auspices of government officials. He also emphasizes the values of equality and fairness in the financing and delivery of care. Conspicuously light in his presentation of the issue is exactly *how* this proposal would increase the quality of care for Americans. He seems to simply assume that it would.

There are different definitions of health care quality. One way of measuring quality is whether patients receive the right diagnosis and the right treatment at the right time. As a practical matter, quality is a function of access to competent and timely professional medical care.

When Professor Hacker does target the quality issue, he misses the mark. He uses the example of Medicare. He asserts, for instance, that "Medicare already shows unique quality advantages over private insurance that would carry over to a new public plan for the non-elderly. Elderly Americans with Medicare report that they have greater access to physicians for routine care and in cases of injury or illness than do the privately insured."[7]

This issue of access deserves a closer examination; for the evidence is not as conclusive as Professor Hacker suggests. According to a recent report in *The New York Times*, a growing number of physicians, particularly internists, are dropping out of Medicare altogether because of low Medicare reimbursement rates and the burden of Medicare paperwork.[8] Moreover, according to the *Times*, a Texas Medical Association survey of that state's doctors found that while 58 percent of Texas doctors accepted new Medicare patients, only 38 percent of primary care doctors did so.[9] Patients go to hospital emergency rooms for a variety of reasons, but one of the reasons is that going to the emergency room is the only way some people can see a doctor at all. According to a study conducted by the National Center for Health Statistics, patients covered by private insurance made fewer visits to hospital emergency rooms and outpatient hospital departments than did patients covered by Medicare.[10]

Likewise, in his references to Medicare's advantages in delivering high-quality care, Professor Hacker cites the work of the Medicare Payment Advisory Commission (MedPAC). But MedPAC makes no such claims about Medicare as a quality leader. In fact, MedPAC warns that Medicare's well-known design deficiencies and its financial problems will certainly inhibit its delivery of high-quality care. In its June 2008 report to Congress, "Reforming the Delivery System," MedPAC states that "Without change, the Medicare program is fiscally unsustainable over the long term and is not designed to produce high-quality care."[11] In his positive description of Medicare as a "quality leader," Professor Hacker also references the work of Karen Davis and Sara Collins, top policy analysts at the Commonwealth Fund, which appeared in the *Health Care Financing Review.* In their article, "Medicare at Forty," however, Davis and Collins conclude that "Medicare needs to move more aggressively *to* become a leader in promoting high-quality, high-efficiency care for Medicare beneficiaries and for all Americans" [emphasis added].[12] This is a somewhat tamer perspective.

[...]

Measuring Quality

Creation of a new government plan is merely a diversion from the core issue that under existing Medicare administrative payment systems—precisely the payment systems that champions of the new government-run plan routinely applaud—inefficiency is richly rewarded and innovation is soundly punished. In the management of back pain, MedPAC provided a clear example: "[T]he Virginia Mason Medical Center in Washington state reported to the Commission that its lower back pain initiative greatly reduced insurance companies' cost for members with lower back pain but, under standard FFS payment rules, decreased the center's revenues."[13]

[…]

Why More Government Spending Does Not Produce Higher Quality

[…]

Simply pumping more money into the current health care arrangements—government programs and employment-based health insurance—is highly unlikely to improve quality of care for patients. The Nelson Rockefeller Institute of Government recently issued a report, "Medicaid and Long-Term Care: New York Compared to 18 Other States," that concludes: "Unfortunately, New York's broad range of services and higher spending have not produced a higher quality of care. The state is about average or slightly above average on measures of quality. The comparisons in this report show that New York has room to improve quality and lower costs."[14] The actuarial firm Milliman, Inc., estimated that 25 percent of hospitalizations for Wyoming's long-term care population were avoidable.[15]

Government Control

Government regulations typically measure process and conformance, not necessarily quality. How regulations can stifle quality improvement is rarely examined. All too often, our systems are "average" rather than "best." Giving government a greater role in regulating providers is not likely to change results. We are not suffering from a lack of regulation in Medicare and Medicaid.

[…]

Federal, state, and local officials are often presented with competing interests, including that providers benefit financially from inefficiencies in the delivery system that so many now oppose. Los Angeles's MLK Hospital remained open for years despite public outrage over high-profile deaths and injuries resulting from sub-standard care and incompetence. A two-tiered system of care persisted for years in Louisiana despite widespread concerns over patient care. The notion that running health care decisions through a government filter will purify the outcome or is more likely to protect the public interest simply does not reflect reality.

Conclusion

Congress is on a fast timetable to overhaul the American health care system. It is closely following President Obama's prescriptions to centralize health care decision-making in Washington. The Senate Finance Committee is expected to consider health care reform legislation in June of 2009.

The President has repeatedly promised Americans that they would be able to keep the health insurance that they have today if they wished to do so. But the proposal to create a new government-run health plan to "compete" with private-sector plans would make such a promise impossible to keep. Instead, the likelihood is that millions of Americans would lose their existing coverage, regardless of their personal preferences in the matter, and be pushed into the new public plan or Medicaid. Moreover, inasmuch as Medicare is the common model for a new government-run health care plan, it is fair to examine Medicare's record on delivery of high-quality health care. Professor Hacker's insistence notwithstanding, Medicare is not a quality leader in health care, and there is also evidence that current enrollees in government-run health plans are having problems with access to health care.

No question: America's $2.4 trillion health care system needs to be reformed. Policymakers at the state and federal levels can work together to increase access to affordable health insurance and improve the quality of care. But destroying the private health insurance of millions of Americans through rigged "competition" with a new public health plan, funded by taxpayer subsidies and artificial pricing, will result in *reduced* choice and competition, *less* innovation, and a *lowering* of overall health care quality. If champions of a single-payer health care system think they have the best option for America, let them offer that option on the floors of the House and Senate for a full and open debate.

Notes

1. Jacob S. Hacker, "Health Care for America: A Proposal for Guaranteed, Affordable Health Care for all Americans Building on Medicare and Employment-Based Insurance," Economic Policy Institute Briefing Paper No. 180, January 11, 2007, p. 1, at http://www.sharedprosperity.org/bp180.html (April 17, 2009).

2. Jacob S. Hacker, "Thinking Big on Health Care," Thinking Big, Thinking Forward: A Conference on America's Economic Future, February 11, 2009, at http://www.ourfuture.org/files/Thinking_Big_Feb_2009_Hacker.pdf (April 17, 2009).

3. Jacob S. Hacker, "Better Medicine," Slate, October 10, 2006, at http://www.slate.com/id/2151269/?nav=tap3 (April 17, 2009).

4. Jacob S. Hacker, "Politics Comes First," posted by CommonHealth, January 18, 2009, at http://www.commonhealth.wbur.org.

5. Ibid.

6. Ibid.

7. Hacker, "The Case for Public Plan Choice in National Health Reform," p. 14.

8. Julie Connelly, "Doctors Are Opting Out of Medicare," *The New York Times*, April 2, 2009.

9. Ibid.

10. Susan M. Schappert and Elizabeth A. Rechsteiner, "Ambulatory Medical Care Utilization Estimates for 2006," National Health Statistics Report No. 8, August 6, 2008, Table 1.

11. Glenn Hackbarth, "Report to the Congress: Reforming the Delivery System," MedPAC, Washington, D.C., June 13, 2008.

12. Karen Davis and Sara R. Collins, "Medicare at Forty," *Health Care Financing Review*, Vol. 27, No. 2 (Winter 2005-2006), p. 61.

13. Hackbarth, "Report to the Congress: Reforming the Delivery System," p. 7 (internal citation omitted).

14. The New York Health Policy Research Center, "Medicaid and Long-Term Care: New York Compared to 18 Other States," prepared for the New York State Department of Health, February 2009, p. 14.

15. Bruce Pyeson, Kathryn Fitch, and Susan Panteley, Medicaid Program Redesign: The Long Term Care and Developmentally Disabled Programs, Milliman, Inc., September 15, 2006, p. 12.

CHAPTER 2

Does the Cost of Universal Health Care Outweigh the Benefits?

US Spending, Services, Price, and Health Compared to the Rest of the World

David Squires and Chloe Anderson

David Squires formerly served as a senior researcher for Commonwealth Fund President David Blumenthal and senior researcher for the organization's International Health Policy and Practice Innovations program. Chloe Anderson is a former research associate in the International Health Policy and Practice Innovations Program at the Commonwealth Fund.

Cross-national comparisons allow us to track the performance of the US health care system, highlight areas of strength and weakness, and identify factors that may impede or accelerate improvement. This analysis is the latest in a series of Commonwealth Fund cross-national comparisons that use health data from the Organization for Economic Cooperation and Development (OECD), as well as from other sources, to assess US health care system spending, supply, utilization, and prices relative to other countries, as well as a limited set of health outcomes.[1,2] Thirteen high-income countries are included: Australia, Canada, Denmark, France, Germany, Japan, Netherlands, New Zealand, Norway, Sweden, Switzerland, the United Kingdom, and the United States. On measures where data are widely available, the value for the median OECD country is also shown. Almost all data are for years prior to the major insurance provisions of the Affordable Care Act; most are for 2013.

Health care spending in the US far exceeds that of other high-income countries, though spending growth has slowed in the US and in most other countries in recent years.[3] Even though the US is the only country without a publicly financed universal health

"U.S. Health Care from a Global Perspective," by David Squires and Chloe Anderson, The Commonwealth Fund, October 2015. Reprinted by permission.

system, it still spends more public dollars on health care than all but two of the other countries. Americans have relatively few hospital admissions and physician visits but are greater users of expensive technologies like magnetic resonance imaging (MRI) machines. Available cross-national pricing data suggest that prices for health care are notably higher in the US, potentially explaining a large part of the higher health spending. In contrast, the US devotes a relatively small share of its economy to social services, such as housing assistance, employment programs, disability benefits, and food security.[4] Finally, despite its heavy investment in health care, the US sees poorer results on several key health outcome measures such as life expectancy and the prevalence of chronic conditions. Mortality rates from cancer are low and have fallen more quickly in the US than in other countries, but the reverse is true for mortality from ischemic heart disease.

Key Findings

The United States Is the Highest Spender on Health Care

Data from the OECD show that the US spent 17.1 percent of its gross domestic product (GDP) on health care in 2013. This was almost 50 percent more than the next-highest spender (France, 11.6% of GDP) and almost double what was spent in the UK (8.8%). US spending per person was equivalent to $9,086 (not adjusted for inflation).

Since 2009, health care spending growth has slowed in the US and most other countries. The real growth rate per capita in the US declined from 2.47 percent between 2003 and 2009 to 1.50 percent between 2009 and 2013. In Denmark and the United Kingdom, the growth rate actually became negative. The timing and cross-national nature of the slowdown suggest a connection to the 2007–2009 global financial crisis and its aftereffects, though additional factors also may be at play.[5]

Private Spending on Health Care Is Highest in the US

In 2013, the average US resident spent $1,074 out-of-pocket on health care, for things like copayments for doctor's office visits and prescription drugs and health insurance deductibles. Only the Swiss spent more at $1,630, while France and the Netherlands spent less than one-fourth as much ($277 and $270, respectively). As for other private health spending, including on private insurance premiums, US spending towered over that of the other countries at $3,442 per capita—more than five times what was spent in Canada ($654), the second-highest spending country.[6]

US Public Spending on Health Care Is High,
Despite Covering Fewer Residents

Public spending on health care amounted to $4,197 per capita in the US in 2013, more than in any other country except Norway ($4,981) and the Netherlands ($4,495), despite the fact that the US was the only country studied that did not have a universal health care system. In the US, about 34 percent of residents were covered by public programs in 2013, including Medicare and Medicaid.[7] By comparison, every resident in the United Kingdom is covered by the public system and spending was $2,802 per capita. Public spending on health care would be even greater in the US if the tax exclusion for employer-sponsored health insurance (amounting to about $250 billion each year) was counted as a public expenditure.[8]

Despite Spending More on Health Care, Americans
Have Fewer Hospital and Physician Visits

The US had fewer practicing physicians in 2013 than in the median OECD country (2.6 versus 3.2 physicians per 1,000 population). With only four per year, Americans also had fewer physician visits than the OECD median (6.5 visits). In contrast, the average Canadian had 7.7 physician visits and the average Japanese resident had 12.9 visits in 2012.

In the US, there were also fewer hospital beds and fewer discharges per capita than in the median OECD country.

Americans Appear to Be Greater Consumers of Medical Technology, Including Diagnostic Imaging and Pharmaceuticals

The US stood out as a top consumer of sophisticated diagnostic imaging technology. Americans had the highest per capita rates of MRI, computed tomography (CT), and positron emission tomography (PET) exams among the countries where data were available. The US and Japan were among the countries with the highest number of these imaging machines.[9]

In addition, Americans were top consumers of prescription drugs. Based on findings from the 2013 Commonwealth Fund International Surveys, adults in the US and New Zealand on average take more prescription drugs (2.2 per adult) than adults in other countries.

Health Care Prices Are Higher in the US Compared with Other Countries

Data published by the International Federation of Health Plans suggest that hospital and physician prices for procedures were highest in the US in 2013.[10] The average price of bypass surgery was $75,345 in the US. This is more than $30,000 higher than in the second-highest country, Australia, where the procedure costs $42,130. According to the same data source, MRI and CT scans were also most expensive in the US. While these pricing data are subject to significant methodological limitations, they illustrate a pattern of significantly higher prices in many areas of US health care.

Other studies have observed high US prices for pharmaceuticals. A 2013 investigation by Kanavos and colleagues created a cross-national price index for a basket of widely used in-patent pharmaceuticals. In 2010, all countries studied had lower prices than the US. In Australia, Canada, and the United Kingdom, prices were about 50 percent lower.[11]

The US Invests the Smallest Share of Its Economy on Social Services

A 2013 study by Bradley and Taylor found that the US spent the least on social services—such as retirement and disability benefits, employment programs, and supportive housing—among the countries studied in this report, at just 9 percent of GDP.[12] Canada, Australia and New Zealand had similarly low rates of spending, while France, Sweden, Switzerland, and Germany devoted roughly twice as large a share of their economy to social services as did the US.

The US was also the only country studied where health care spending accounted for a greater share of GDP than social services spending. In aggregate, US health and social services spending rank near the middle of the pack.

Despite Its High Spending on Health Care, the US Has Poor Population Health

On several measures of population health, Americans had worse outcomes than their international peers. The US had the lowest life expectancy at birth of the countries studied, at 78.8 years in 2013, compared with the OECD median of 81.2 years. Additionally, the US had the highest infant mortality rate among the countries studied, at 6.1 deaths per 1,000 live births in 2011; the rate in the OECD median country was 3.5 deaths.

The prevalence of chronic diseases also appeared to be higher in the US. The 2014 Commonwealth Fund International Health Policy Survey found that 68 percent of US adults age 65 or older had at least two chronic conditions. In other countries, this figure ranged from 33 percent (UK) to 56 percent (Canada).[13]

A 2013 report from the Institute of Medicine reviewed the literature about the health disadvantages of Americans relative to residents of other high-income countries. It found the US performed poorly on several important determinants of health.[14] More than a third of adults in the US were obese in 2012, a rate that was about 15 percent higher than the next-highest country, New Zealand.

The US had one of the lowest smoking rates in 2013 but one of the highest rates of tobacco consumption in the 1960s and 1970s. This earlier period of heavy tobacco use may still be contributing to relatively worse health outcomes among older US adults.[15] Other potential contributors to the United States' health disadvantage include the large number of uninsured, as well as differences in lifestyle, environment, and rates of accidents and violence.

The Institute of Medicine found that poorer health in the US was not simply the result of economic, social, or racial and ethnic disadvantages—even well-off, nonsmoking, nonobese Americans appear in worse health than their counterparts abroad.

The US Performs Well on Cancer Care but Has High Rates of Mortality from Heart Disease and Amputations as a Result of Diabetes

One area where the US appeared to have comparatively good health outcomes was cancer care. A 2015 study by Stevens et al. found that mortality rates from cancer in the US were lower and had declined faster between 1995 and 2007 than in most industrialized countries.[16] Other research based on survival rates also suggests that US cancer care is above average, though these studies are disputed on methodological grounds.[17]

The opposite trend appears for ischemic heart disease, where the US had among the highest mortality rates in 2013—128 per 100,000 population compared with 95 in the median OECD country. Since 1995, mortality rates have fallen significantly in all countries as a result of improved treatment and changes in risk factors.[18] However, this decline was less pronounced in the US, where rates declined from 225 to 128 deaths per 100,000 population—considerably less than countries like Denmark, where rates declined from 242 to 71 deaths per 100,000 population.

The US also had high rates of adverse outcomes from diabetes, with 17.1 lower extremity amputations per 100,000 population in 2011. Rates in Sweden, Australia and the UK were less than one-third as high.

Discussion

Health care spending in the US far exceeds that in other countries, despite a global slowdown in spending growth in recent years. At 17.1 percent of GDP, the US devotes at least 50 percent more of its economy to health care than do other countries. Even public spending on health care, on a per capita basis, is higher in the US than in most other countries with universal public coverage.

How can we explain the higher US spending? In line with previous studies,[19] the results of this analysis suggest that the excess is likely driven by greater utilization of medical technology and higher prices, rather than use of routine services, such as more frequent visits to physicians and hospitals.

High health care spending has far-reaching consequences in the US economy, contributing to wage stagnation, personal bankruptcy, and budget deficits and creating a competitive disadvantage relative to other nations.[20] One potential consequence of high health spending is that it may crowd out other forms of social spending that support health. In the US, health care spending substantially outweighs spending on social services. This imbalance may contribute to the country's poor health outcomes. A growing body of evidence suggests that social services play an important role in shaping health trajectories and mitigating health disparities.[21,22] Additional cross-national research is needed to better understand the relationship between social services and health, as well as other health determinants like lifestyle and environment.

New care models that reward health care providers based on their patient population's health outcomes (e.g., accountable care organizations) are an interesting development. Such accountability could create a business case for health care providers to invest in certain social services or other nonclinical interventions, if doing so would be a cost-effective way to improve patients' health.[23] Over the long term, such a strategy could potentially alter the current balance between health and social services spending.

Notes

1. D. Squires, "The Global Slowdown in Health Care Spending," *Journal of the American Medical Association,* Aug. 6, 2014 312(5):485–86; D. Squires, *Explaining High Health Care Spending in the United States: An International Comparison of Supply, Utilization, Prices, and Quality* (New York: The Commonwealth Fund, May 2012); D. Squires, *The U.S. Health System in Perspective: A Comparison of Twelve Industrialized Nations* (New York: The Commonwealth Fund, July 2011); G. F. Anderson and D. Squires, *Measuring the U.S. Health Care System: A Cross-National Comparison* (New York: The Commonwealth Fund, June 2010); G. F. Anderson and B. K. Frogner, "Health Spending in OECD Countries: Obtaining Value per Dollar," *Health Affairs,* Nov./Dec. 2008 27(6):1718–27; G. F. Anderson, B. K. Frogner, and U. E. Reinhardt, "Health Spending in OECD Countries in 2004: An Update," *Health Affairs,* Sept./Oct. 2007 26(5):1481–89; G. F. Anderson, P. S. Hussey, B. K. Frogner et al., "Health Spending in the United States and the Rest of the Industrialized World," *Health Affairs,* July/Aug. 2005 24(4):903–14; U. E. Reinhardt, P. S. Hussey, and G. F. Anderson, "U.S. Health Care Spending in an International Context," *Health Affairs,* May/June 2004 23(3):10–25; G. F. Anderson, U. E. Reinhardt, P. S. Hussey et al., "It's the Prices, Stupid: Why the United States Is So Different from Other Countries," *Health Affairs,* May/June 2003, 22(3):89–105; U. E. Reinhardt, P. S. Hussey, and G. F. Anderson, "Cross-National Comparisons of Health Systems Using OECD Data, 1999," *Health Affairs,* May/ June 2002 21(3):169–81; G. F. Anderson and P. S. Hussey, "Comparing Health System Performance in OECD Countries," *Health Affairs,* May/June 2001 20(3):219–32; G. F. Anderson, J. Hurst, P. S. Hussey et al., "Health Spending and Outcomes: Trends in OECD Countries, 1960–1998," *Health Affairs,* May/ June 2000 19(3):150–57; and G. F. Anderson and J. P. Poullier, "Health Spending, Access, and Outcomes: Trends in Industrialized Countries," *Health Affairs,* May/ June 1999 18(3):178–92.

2. Unlike the Fund's Mirror, Mirror on the Wall series, this report does not attempt to assess overall health system performance, or rank health systems across various metrics. See: K. Davis, K. Stremikis, C. Schoen, and D. Squires, *Mirror, Mirror on the Wall, 2014 Update: How the U.S. Health Care System Compares Internationally* (New York: The Commonwealth Fund, June 2014).

3. Organization for Economic Cooperation and Development, *OECD Health Data 2015* (Paris: OECD, June 2015).

4. E. H. Bradley and L. A. Taylor, *The American Health Care Paradox: Why Spending More Is Getting Us Less* (New York: Public Affairs, 2013).

5. Squires, "Global Slowdown," 2014.

6. Because of data limitations in several countries, the breakdown of health spending by source of financing is for current spending only, meaning it excludes capital formation of health care providers. In most countries, those amounts range between 2 percent and 7 percent of total health spending.

7. U.S. Census Bureau, *Health Insurance in the United States: 2013—Tables & Figures,* 2014.

8. Congressional Budget Office, *Options for Reducing The Deficit: 2014 to 2023* (Washington, D.C.: CBO, Nov. 2013).

9. It should be noted that, despite the comparatively high levels of use in the U.S., growth in medical imaging appears to have leveled off in recent years after surging through much of the 2000s. The slowdown has been attributed to patient cost-sharing, prior authorization, best-practice guidelines, and other strategies to reduce potentially unnecessary utilization. See D. W. Lee and F. Levy, "The Sharp Slowdown in Growth of Medical Imaging: An Early Analysis Suggests Combination of Policies Was the Cause," *Health Affairs,* Aug. 2012 31(8):1876–84.

10. International Federation of Health Plans, 2013 Comparative Price Report.

11. P. Kanavos, A. Ferrario, S. Vandoros et al., "Higher U.S. Branded Drug Prices and Spending Compared to Other Countries May Stem Partly from Quick Uptake of New Drugs," *Health Affairs,* April 2013 32(4):753–61.

12. Bradley and Taylor, *American Health Care Paradox,* 2013.

13. Chronic conditions included hypertension or high blood pressure, heart disease, diabetes, lung problems, mental health problems, cancer, and joint pain/arthritis. See Commonwealth Fund 2014 International Health Policy Survey of Older Adults.

14. J. D. Freeman, S. Kadiyala, J. F. Bell et al., "The Causal Effect of Health Insurance on Utilization and Outcomes in Adults: A Systematic Review of US Studies," *Medical Care,* 2008 46(10):1023–32; and S. H. Woolf and L. Aron (eds.), *U.S. Health in International Perspective: Shorter Lives, Poorer Health* (Washington, D.C.: National Academies Press, 2013).

15. Woolf and Aron (eds.), *U.S. Health in International Perspective,* 2013.

16. W. Stevens, T. J. Philipson, Z. M. Khan et al., "Cancer Mortality Reductions Were Greatest Among Countries Where Cancer Care Spending Rose the Most, 1995–2007," *Health Affairs,* April 2015 34(4):562–70.

17. T. Philipson, M. Eber, D. N. Lakdawalla et al., "An Analysis of Whether Higher Health Care Spending in the United States Versus Europe Is 'Worth It' in the Case of Cancer," *Health Affairs,* April 2012 31(4):667–75; S. Soneji and J. Yang, "New Analysis Reexamines the Value of Cancer Care in the United States Compared to Western Europe," *Health Affairs,* March 2015 34(3):390- 97; D. Goldman, D. Lakdawalla, and T. Philipson, "Mortality Versus Survival in International Comparisons of Cancer Care," *Health Affairs Blog,* March 20, 2015; and H. G. Welch and E. Fisher, "Revisiting Mortality Versus Survival in International Comparisons of Cancer Care," *Health Affairs Blog,* April 1, 2015.

18. Organization for Economic Cooperation and Development, *Cardiovascular Disease and Diabetes: Policies for Better Health and Quality of Care* (Paris: OECD, June 2015).

19. Squires, *Explaining High Health Care Spending,* 2012; Anderson, Frogner, and Reinhardt, "Health Spending in OECD Countries," 2007; M. J. Laugesen and S. A. Glied, "Higher Fees Paid to U.S. Physicians Drive Higher Spending for Physician Services Compared to Other Countries," *Health Affairs,* Sept. 2011 30(9):1647–56.

20. D. I. Auerbach and A. L. Kellermann, "A Decade of Health Care Cost Growth Has Wiped Out Real Income Gains for an Average U.S. Family," *Health Affairs,* Sept. 2011 30(9):1630–36; D. Blumenthal and D. Squires, "Do Health Care Costs Fuel Economic Inequality in the United States?" *The Commonwealth Fund Blog,* Sept. 9, 2014; D. U. Himmelstein, D. Thorne, E. Warren et al., "Medical Bankruptcy in the United States, 2007: Results of a National Study," *American Journal of Medicine,* Aug. 2009 122(8):741–46; RAND Health, *How Does Growth in Health Care Costs Affect the American Family?* (Santa Monica, Calif.: RAND, 2011); and T. Johnson, *Healthcare Costs and U.S. Competitiveness* (New York: Council on Foreign Relations, March 2012).

21. M. Avendano and I. Kawachi, "Why Do Americans Have Shorter Life Expectancy and Worse Health Than Do People in Other High-Income Countries?" *Annual Review of Public Health,* March 2014 35:307–25; and Bradley and Taylor, *American Health Care Paradox,* 2013.

22. E. H. Bradley, B. R. Elkins, J. Herrin et al., "Health and Social Services Expenditures: Associations with Health Outcomes," *BMJ Quality & Safety,* published online March 29, 2011.

23. D. Bachrach, H. Pfister, K. Wallis et al., *Addressing Patients' Social Needs: An Emerging Business Case for Provider Investment* (New York: The Commonwealth Fund, May 2014).

"Medicare for All" Would Not Solve the Problem of Rising Health Care Costs

David Hogberg

David Hogberg, PhD, is a health care policy expert and former senior fellow and senior policy analyst at the National Center for Public Policy Research.

In mid-2006, the governor of Massachusetts, Mitt Romney, succeeded in passing his health care reform through the Massachusetts legislature. This ignited a debate on health care policy in the US that shows no signs of subsiding. From the governors, to members of Congress, to presidential candidates, it seems that every politician and his brother has some type of health care plan. Newspapers, TV shows and the blogosphere are filled with discussion of health care reform.

In August 2006, the Pew Research Center for the People and the Press found that 90 percent of respondents to an opinion poll viewed health care affordability as either a big problem or a very big problem. A more recent Pew survey found that 68 percent of respondents said reducing health care costs should be a priority for President Bush and Congress. Chances are good the health care issue will loom large in the public mind for the remainder of the decade.

The inevitable question: What type of health care policy should the US pursue?

One proposal, popular among many on the political left, is "Medicare for All," a proposal that would put most, if not all, Americans under the auspices of the government-run health insurance program for the elderly and disabled. Before the US adopts such a system, it is important to evaluate the claims of

"'Medicare for All': Universal Health Care Would Not Solve the Problem of Rising Health Care Costs," by David Hogberg, Adjunct Fellow, National Center for Public Policy Research, September 2007. Reprinted by permission.

the proponents of Medicare for All. This study addresses this by examining the three oft-repeated claims of Medicare for All proponents: 1) that Medicare for All will save on administrative costs; 2) that Medicare for All will provide quality care; and 3) that Medicare for All will be affordable.

Before addressing those claims, a brief description of Medicare and Medicare for All is needed.

Medicare and Medicare for All

Medicare is the government-run health insurance program that covers most Americans over age 65, those under 65 with certain disabilities, and those with permanent kidney failure. Established by Congress and President Lyndon Johnson in 1965, Medicare initially consisted of Part A, which covers hospital costs, and Part B, which covers doctor's visits and other outpatient services. In 1997, Congress and President Bill Clinton created Medicare Part C, which allows seniors to receive their Medicare benefits through a private insurer. In 2003, Congress and President George W. Bush created Medicare Part D, which covers prescription drugs.

The bulk of Medicare is funded through a combination of payroll taxes and general revenues, with the remainder being funded through premiums, deductibles, and other out-of-pocket expenses. Medicare is administered by the Center for Medicare and Medicaid Services (CMS), formerly the Health Care Financing Administration. Although seniors can opt out of Medicare, to do so they must, under federal law, forego their Social Security benefits. At present, about 42.5 million beneficiaries are enrolled in Medicare, 35.8 million elderly and 6.7 million disabled.

Medicare for All would entail enrolling most, if not all, Americans in the same program that the elderly and disabled currently have access to. Most proposals would open Medicare to any American who wanted to join, while still allowing those Americans who did not want to join Medicare to purchase private insurance. Whether the government will provide funds for the purchase of private insurance is less clear.

For example, Senator Edward Kennedy (D-MA) states,

For those who prefer private insurance, we will offer comparable coverage under the same range of private insurance plans already available to Congress. I can think of nothing more cynical or hypocritical than a Member of Congress who gives a speech denouncing health care for all, then goes to his doctor for a visit paid for by the Federal Employees Health Benefit Plan.

Under its Medicare for All proposal, the Medicare Rights Center says private insurers can "remain in the business of providing people with coverage so long as it is at least as good as Medicare offers, and they must compete." While Medicare for All may not require every American to join Medicare per se, it will force private insurance to provide all customers with benefits similar to Medicare. In effect, every American will have coverage that is at least equal to that provided by Medicare.

Paying for Medicare for All will, naturally, require tax increases. According to Senator Kennedy, "As we implement this reform, financing must be a shared responsibility. All will benefit, and all should contribute. Payroll taxes should be part of the financing, but so should general revenues, to make the financing as progressive as possible."

The main reason that the political left wishes to dub its universal health insurance scheme Medicare for All is the belief that that naming the system after Medicare will make it more palatable to voters.

For example, liberal pundit Paul Krugman states:

A system in which the government provides universal health insurance is often referred to as "single payer," but I like Ted Kennedy's slogan "Medicare for All." It reminds voters that America already has a highly successful, popular single-payer program, albeit only for the elderly.

But how successful is Medicare? And, by extension, how successful would a system of Medicare for All really be? The remainder of this analysis examines the claims of Medicare for All proponents.

[...]

Affordability

Looking over the speeches and press releases of the advocates of Medicare for All, the word "affordable" appears again and again. Representative Stark says that his legislation will "provide all Americans with access to affordable, comprehensive, quality health coverage." Senator Kennedy states that the battle to win Medicare for All is "the battle to make health care affordable and available to all our people." Presumably, they believe Medicare for All would be more affordable than our current system.

Our current health care system does seem to be increasingly unaffordable. Since 1999, premiums for private insurance have risen an average of 9.9 percent annually, far outpacing inflation and forcing many employers to drop insurance coverage. From 2000-2005, health care expenditures as a percentage of gross domestic product (GDP) grew from 13.8 percent to 16 percent, a total increase of 16 percent. As a percentage of GDP, private health insurance grew 19.6 percent during that period, while total private spending (private insurance plus out-of-pocket spending) grew 13 percent. A recent report from CMS stated that by 2016 health care expenses would account for 20 percent of GDP. Health care costs, it seems, are exploding.

Would Medicare for All control them? Senator Kennedy certainly thinks so. He states that Medicare for All,

> will be financed by a combination of payroll taxes and general revenues. Eighty-five percent of the financing will come from payroll taxes and 15% from general revenues. A preliminary estimate of the payroll tax financing necessary will be a payment of 7% of payroll by businesses and 1.7% by workers. By comparison, businesses providing coverage today spend an average of 13% of payroll to cover their workers.

Thus, it seems a payroll tax of 8.7 percent would provide Medicare coverage for all. However, as the press release makes clear, that is only to add everyone *under* 65 to Medicare. If the

3.2 percent payroll tax already in effect that pays for beneficiaries over 65 is included, the total payroll tax for Medicare would be 11.9 percent. Furthermore, it's not clear where Senator Kennedy gets the figure of 13 percent of payroll for businesses that provide coverage. The most recent Employee Benefit Compensation Survey found that all insurance benefits (health, life, and disability) paid by business amounted to 8.1 percent of compensation.

There seems to be little in the way of cost savings in Medicare premiums, either.

Medicare premiums have fared only modestly better than those of private insurance, rising an average of 8.9 percent from 1999-2007. It is doubtful that even that modestly slower rate of increase will endure in the future. The small premium increases of 1999 and 2000 were due to cost controls put on Medicare in the 1997 Balanced Budget Act, controls that clearly did not last. Second, the slower rate of increase in 2007 is largely accounted for by the fact that the Bush Administration decided to cover a larger part of Part B costs with general revenues. Had Part B costs been covered by an increase in premiums, then premiums would have increased over 11 percent in 2007. For 2008, premiums are predicted to rise 17 percent.

While Medicare fails at keeping premiums costs down, it is also consuming a larger portion of GDP. From 2000-2005, Medicare's share of GDP grew 17 percent. That's less than the 19.6 percent of private insurance, but higher than 13 percent of total private spending, which includes out-of-pocket payments.

The fiscal future of Medicare itself is bleak. The Medicare Trustees report notes that, by 2018, revenues for Part A will only be sufficient to cover 80 percent of its costs. By 2080, revenues will only cover 29 percent of costs. "Closing deficits of this magnitude," the report warns, "will require very substantial increases in tax revenues and/or reductions in expenditures." The prospects for Part B and Part D are not much better, with the report stating that revenues for those parts will "have to increase rapidly to match expected expenditure growth under current law." From 2005-

2080, the report predicts, Medicare's share of GDP will rise from 2.7 percent to 11 percent.

Why anyone would want to put every American in a program that is already nearing fiscal collapse is perplexing, to say the least.

Proponents of Medicare for All would probably respond that savings would be achieved by reducing administrative costs. As shown above, such savings are dubious. It is also important to note that administrative costs are one-time savings. That is, the administrators that are not longer needed are let go only once; continuous savings are not achieved by removing administrators every year.

Reducing administrative costs does nothing to solve the main driver of Medicare's costs, which is that Medicare is a third-party payer system. This means that a third-party, in this case the government, pays for most of the care health care professionals provide. Patients believe "someone else" is paying the bill. As a result, they have little incentive to restrain their demand for health care. This leads to an ever-rising demand for health care, and rising demand leads to higher costs.

Early research failed to confirm that Medicare was responsible for rising health care costs. Rather, it laid the blame for rising health care costs at the feet of technological advances. New research from Professor Amy Finkelstein of the Massachusetts Institute of Technology, however, suggests that Medicare is more culpable than initially thought.

Finkelstein realized that Medicare's effect would not be uniform across the country. Rather, it would have a greater effect on total health care spending in regions where few seniors had private health insurance before the introduction of Medicare and a lesser effect on regions where many seniors had health insurance. Controlling for regional differences, she found "that the introduction of Medicare is associated with a 37 percent increase in hospital spending over its first five years." Using a "back of the envelope" calculation, she estimates that the "overall spread of health insurance may therefore be able to explain half of the six-fold increase in real per capita health spending" between 1950 and 1990. Much of the spread of health insurance can be attributed to Medicare since "Medicare's introduction constituted the single largest change in health insurance coverage in American history."

Since Medicare contributes heavily to rising health care costs, it would only be a matter of time before the cost of Medicare for All exceeded any savings from lower administrative costs, leaving us where we are today with health care costs consuming 16 percent of GDP. To see how long that would take, the amount of health care costs for 2005, about $1.98 trillion, was reduced by the largest estimated amount of administrative cost savings, $440 billion (see section on administrative costs above). That number was then increased annually by average growth rate of Medicare over the last decade, seven percent. GDP was increased annually by the average growth rate of GDP over the last decade, 3.2 percent.

It takes only eight years, until 2013, before health care expenditures again reach 16 percent of GDP.

For a variety of reasons health care costs under Medicare for All will almost surely reach 16 percent of GDP much faster. First, the $440 billion figure of administrative costs savings is almost surely too large, as the section in this paper on administrative costs shows. Second, under Medicare for All, the uninsured will have greater access to health care, and since the government will be perceived as paying for it, they are far more likely to use it, leading to an increase in demand for health care. Third, those individuals with high-deductible insurance policies will now be forced into an insurance program with either much lower deductibles or no deductibles at all. They, too, will now have incentive to increase their demand for health care resulting in upward pressure on costs.

The current Medicare system is ineffective at reducing health care costs. Indeed, it is a major cause of the escalation of such costs. There is no reason to think that Medicare for All would be any different.

Conclusion

In a recent article in the *New York Review of Books*, Paul Krugman and Robin Wells state that "the obvious way to make the U.S. health care system more efficient is to make it more like the systems of other advanced countries, and more like the most efficient parts of our own system ... the core of the system would be government insurance—'Medicare for all.'" The problem with this analysis is that Medicare isn't one of those efficient parts.

Medicare is ineffective at controlling costs. Wasteful spending is a particularly acute problem, leading to as much as one dollar in five being spent on health care that is of no value and possibly harmful. This stems from the fact that Medicare is largely a third-party payer system, insulating patients from the cost of their care and thereby shielding them from the need to make decisions about what care is necessary.

Putting all Americans under Medicare would not solve this nation's problem of rising health care costs.

State Politicians Take the Lead in Providing Universal Health Care

Pauline Bartolone

Pauline Bartolone is a Sacramento Correspondent for California Healthline. *She has been a radio and print journalist for 15 years, frequently contributing to NPR.*

As the nation's Republican leaders huddle to reconsider their plans to "repeal and replace" the nation's health law, advocates for universal health coverage press on in California, armed with renewed political will and a new set of proposals.

Organized labor and two lawmakers are leading the charge for a single, government-financed program for everyone in the state. Another legislator wants to create a commission that would weigh the best options for a system to cover everyone. And Democratic Lt. Gov. Gavin Newsom, who hopes to become the next governor, has suggested building on employer-based health care to plug holes in existing coverage.

The proposals are fueled both by a fear of losing gains under the Affordable Care Act and a sense that the law doesn't go far enough toward covering everyone and cutting costs.

But health policy experts say that creating any type of universal health plan would face enormous political and fiscal challenges—and that if it happens at all, it could take years.

"There are different ways to get there," says Jonathan Oberlander, professor of social medicine and health policy at the University of North Carolina. "None of them is easy."

The most specific California proposal comes from state Sens. Ricardo Lara (D-Bell Gardens) and Toni Atkins (D-San Diego), co-authors of legislation that would take steps toward creating one publicly financed "single-payer" program.

The bill, co-sponsored by the California Nurses Association, would aim for something like a system of "Medicare for all" in which the government, not insurers, provides payments and sets coverage rules.

Lara said the approach would get California closer to a system "that covers more and costs less."

The bill's authors haven't announced how the program would be funded. And that's where the biggest obstacle lies, said Oberlander: It would largely uproot California's present system, in which roughly half of coverage is sponsored by employers.

If "you're going to take health insurance largely out of the market, you're going to disconnect it from employers," he said. "Then you have to make up all the financing that you're going to lose."

There's no way to make up for those lost employer contributions other than to introduce "very visible taxes," Oberlander said. And that's not the only reason why a single payer plan would be controversial. "A lot of people are satisfied with what they have," he said.

The trade group for insurers in California does not support the single-payer idea.

"A single-payer system would make the quality of our health care worse, not better," said Charles Bacchi, president and CEO of the California Association of Health Plans. "We've made substantial progress in expanding and increasing access to and quality of care—this step backwards would be particularly devastating for Californians."

Many conservatives oppose the single-payer approach. "We have come to value and expect a health care system that has private-sector market elements," said Lanhee Chen, a fellow at the Hoover Institution and former chief policy adviser to former Massachusetts governor Mitt Romney.

A single-payer system would need federal approval and likely have to overcome other bureaucratic hurdles even if approved in the state. As it stands, no state has such a system. Perhaps the best-known effort to create one was in Vermont, but it failed in 2014 after officials there couldn't figure out how to finance it.

Single-payer proposals have been put forth many times in the California Legislature since 2003, and all have hit roadblocks.

One bill, carried by former state senator Sheila Kuehl several years ago and passed by the state Legislature, would have created a payroll tax to help fund a program costing about $200 billion each year. That measure and a similar bill were vetoed by then-governor Arnold Schwarzenegger, who cited financial concerns.

Kuehl, now a Los Angeles County supervisor, said the time is as good as ever to reintroduce a proposal like single-payer because many people fear losing coverage under Republican proposals being discussed in Washington, DC.

"The ACA created more familiarity with being insured," said Kuehl. "They've recognized the value."

Other observers say attempts to expand access should not undermine efforts to preserve insurance gains under Obamacare. The threat to Medicaid or private insurance access is still real, they say.

"California should explore all options, [but] we should not do that if it means withdrawing support for protecting the ACA," said Jerry Kominski, director of the UCLA Center for Health Policy Research. "It would take decades to get back to where we are now," he said.

In an interview with California Healthline, California Gov. Jerry Brown emphasized that financing a single-payer system would be a major challenge. Although he said he would entertain a conversation about a single-payer system, he did not say whether he would endorse creating one.

For one thing, it would require a new tax, which would have to be approved either by a two-thirds majority vote in the state legislature or a simple-majority popular vote, he said. Even with the current Democratic supermajority, Brown said, there are always a few "outliers" who wouldn't support raising new revenues.

Brown leaves office in 2018, however, and Newsom, who hopes to succeed him, is looking into a creating a plan for universal coverage that would be an alternative to a single-payer system.

One option, according to Newsom's office, would be to use as a model the Healthy San Francisco program he introduced in 2007 as mayor. The city has used a combination of public money and contributions from employers and enrollees to plug holes in coverage and make primary care accessible to nearly everyone.

Newsom has acknowledged, however, that the San Francisco approach would not necessarily work in every county and said he is open to other possibilities.

Using that model to expand health care statewide has some political advantages, Oberlander said, because it builds on the "status quo rather than radically restructuring" the current system.

Another California lawmaker proposes to keep the conversation going about universal health care, at least, by creating a commission that would make various recommendations to policymakers.

"We have to be able to move on multiple tracks at once," said Assemblyman Rob Bonta (D-Oakland), who is carrying the bill to create the Health Care for All commission, which would convene in 2018.

The debate in Washington could actually produce some surprising opportunities for California and other states. The feds might, for instance, approve waivers to allow other types of experimentation within states. Some Republicans favor an approach in which each state decides on its own coverage system, within certain limits.

That could mean a retraction of coverage in some states, but in California it might open the door to a new model.

"It is possible that some liberal-leaning states are going to do things that we didn't think possible before," Oberlander said.

Bernie Sanders's Single-Payer Health Care Plan Is a Total Disaster

Robert E. Moffit

Robert E. Moffit is a senior fellow at the Heritage Foundation's Center for Health Policy Studies.

Americans face a stark choice on what their health care will look like in the future.

They can adopt a government-run health-care system, financed by new and heavy federal taxation, with federal officials making all the key decisions about medical benefits and services. Or, they can adopt a system in which individuals control health-care dollars and decisions, including the kinds of health plans, benefits and treatments that best suit their needs.

Option one, commonly referred to as a "single payer system," makes health care a government monopoly. Option two, based on personal choice, relies on voluntary collaboration and competition among plans and providers to control health-care costs.

Today, we have neither.

What we have is a highly bureaucratic system: one in which the government controls financing for roughly half of US health care; one in which personal choice and competition are rapidly declining; one in which the health-care costs are excessive. Additionally, federal officials are exercising detailed regulatory control over health plans, benefits and even the practice of medicine itself.

Despite President Obama's insistence that Obamacare would not be a government "takeover" of health care, hardly any component of American health care today, courtesy of Obamacare, is insulated from federal regulation and control. Given the general direction of current policy, the trajectory is toward a single-payer system, not away from it.

"Why Bernie Sanders' Single Payer Health Care Plan Is a Total Disaster," by Robert E. Moffit, The Heritage Foundation, September 14, 2017. Reprinted by permission.

Sen. Bernie Sanders, with the cosponsorship of sixteen Senate Democrats, has decided to give the current drift to a government monopoly a giant shove by introducing "The Medicare for All Act of 2017." The bill would replace private health insurance, including employer-sponsored health insurance, with a new and expanded version of the traditional Medicare program.

Rep. John Conyers has already introduced a similar "Medicare for All" bill, cosponsored by 117 House Democrats, more than half of all Democrats in the lower chamber.

Meanwhile, on the West Coast, liberal politicians in California are pushing a statewide "single-payer program." If enacted, the Healthy California Act would displace existing private- and employer-based coverage, as well as Medicare and Medicaid. It would also impose a new 15 percent payroll tax to help cover its estimated annual cost of $400 billion.

Economists and health-policy specialists will spend the next few weeks and months analyzing Sanders' bill. At the end of that process, we should have a pretty clear idea of how this particular proposal will affect doctors, patients and taxpayers.

But we can already predict some of the economic consequences, at least in general terms. That's because imposition of a government health-care monopoly—be it in the form of the Medicare fee-for-service system, the British National Health Service or the Canadian health system—has certain economic features in common.

First, such a system will rely on broad-based taxation, usually in the form of some sort of payroll tax. For example, liberals in Colorado pushed a single-payer initiative in 2016 to be financed by a 10 percent payroll tax, but it failed at the ballot box. Sen. Sanders has proposed a number of "options" to finance his proposal: a 7.5 percent payroll tax on employers, plus a 4 percent "income-based premium" on all Americans, the elimination of the tax breaks on employer-sponsored health insurance, and a series of new taxes on the wealthy.

Last year, Sanders proposed a more modest 6.2 percent employer payroll tax, plus a 2.2 percent universal income tax, as new taxes on "the rich." A 2016 analysis of that proposal by Emory University Professor Kenneth Thorpe concluded:

> The new tax burden would vary dramatically by income. Low-income working families would pay 2.2 percent of taxable income and face a 6.2 percent reduction in wages traced to the employer payroll tax. Individuals and families earning over $250,000 would face a 40 percent increase in taxes to finance the plan and pay for most of the new costs of the plan.

Second, the program costs will surely outrun the official projections. In his analysis of the earlier version of Sanders' bill, Thorpe estimated that the program's cost would average $2.5 trillion a year, "creating an average of over $1 trillion per year financing shortfall." Such a program deficit, Thorpe observed, would require even higher taxes: "To fund the program, payroll and income taxes would have to increase from a combined 8.4 percent in the Sanders plan to 20 percent while also retaining all remaining tax increases on capital gains, increased marginal tax rates, the estate tax and eliminating tax expenditures."

Alternatively, of course, government officials, under such a program, could set and enforce tough health-care budgets. In practice, exercises in government cost control often take the form of old-fashioned price controls or periodic payment cuts to doctors, hospitals or other medical professionals.

The little problem, of course, is that payment reductions for medical services always affect the patients who need those services. Cost control through budgetary limitations or medical-payment cuts typically reduces the access that patients have to treatment, starting with progressively longer waiting lists.

Third, the program will not be a model of simplicity. Sanders insists that the beauty of his proposal is that it will simplify American health care. This is nonsense. There is nothing simple about Medicare, and the nature of the diverse demand for medical services guarantees its regulatory complexity.

Government officials cannot control the demand for medical services; they can only control the supply of medical goods and services. In practice, this means that government officials must determine what kind of care patients get, how they get it, under what circumstances they get it, and how those services will be "priced." (They don't negotiate prices; they fix them.)

There is nothing "simple" about any of this. The Medicare program, with its tens of thousands of pages of rules and regulations and guidelines, demonstrates that painful fact daily to any Medicare patient struggling with a Medicare claims denial or any doctor or any other medical professional wrestling with Medicare paperwork. Meanwhile, forget personal freedom.

Not surprisingly, the Senate Republicans' abysmal failure to enact a health-reform bill has been the main catalyst for the renewed vitality of Sanders' program. His proposal can no longer be dismissed as a product of the far Left. Sen. Elizabeth Warren recently declared that the "progressives" are now the "heart and soul" of the Democratic Party, and the recent embrace of the Sanders' health-policy agenda by senior Senate Democrats and a majority of House Democrats reflects that fact. In her interview with the *Wall Street Journal*, Warren said that, "Now it's time for the next step. And the next step is single payer."

Congressional liberals have a clear vision of health care. They know just where they want to take America. Their agenda is based on heavier taxation, higher federal spending, larger government programs and ever greater government control over the economy.

Congressional conservatives need to offer America something better: a positive vision of health reform based on personal freedom, choice and voluntary collaboration. They need to get back to work and back in the game.

The Case for Universal Health Care

Kao-Ping Chua

Kao-Ping Chua is a practicing general pediatrician and health services researcher.

Over the last few decades, the United States has witnessed skyrocketing health care costs. Health insurance premiums have been rising on average by double-digit percentage points over the past five years, a rate of increase that is 2-3 times the rate of inflation.[1] Because of these out-of-control health care costs, there has been a steep rise in the number of uninsured Americans. Currently, more than 45 million Americans lack any form of health insurance, and millions more are "underinsured"—they have insurance but lack adequate financial protection from health care costs.

While this problem was formerly a problem confined to low-income Americans, more and more middle-class citizens are becoming directly affected by the problem.

In the face of rising health care costs, fewer employers are able to provide their workers with health insurance; the percentage of employers offering health insurance dropped from 69% in 2000 to 60% in 2005. Even if employers are able to provide health insurance benefits, the trend is towards providing high-deductible insurance that covers an ever-shrinking percentage of health care costs.[1] The net result is that more and more employed middle-class Americans find themselves with low-quality or no access to health care.

The erosion of employer-based coverage has been partially offset by increased enrollment in Medicaid, which is designed to provide a safety-net for the lowest income Americans.[2] However, Medicaid has recently been the subject of relentless funding cuts by cash-strapped states and Congressional representatives who are ideologically opposed to welfare programs. As the program

"The Case for Universal Health Care," by Kao-Ping Chua, American Medical Student Association. Reprinted by permission.

continues to be slashed, it is certain that Medicaid will not be able to offset the losses in employer-based insurance, resulting in more and more uninsured individuals.

Health insecurity is at an all-time high. In a time when thousands of people lose their health insurance every day, when health care is becoming elusive to even well-to-do Americans, and when any person is just one pink slip away from becoming uninsured, it becomes clear that health care for all is not just important to achieve, but imperative.

[...]

The Economic Case for Universal Health Care

The central question surrounding the economic case for universal health care is whether achieving health care for all is financially feasible. The answer to this question comes in three parts:

- How much would it cost to achieve universal health care?
- What are the costs of not achieving universal health care?
- Do the costs of achieving universal health care outweigh the benefits?

How Much Would It Cost to Achieve Universal Health Care?

There a number of costs involved with achieving universal health care.[3,4]

- The additional health care that would be used by the uninsured if they had insurance: The Institute of Medicine estimated that this would amount to $34-$69 billion per year, depending on whether the benefits package offered to the uninsured offered public insurance-level benefits (e.g. Medicaid or S-CHIP) or private insurance-level benefits. Note that this number assumes "no structural changes in the systems of health care financing or delivery, average scope of benefits, or provider payment."[3]
- The cost of covering the out-of-pocket costs the uninsured currently pay: The uninsured pay 35% of health care costs

out-of-pocket, compared to 20% for the insured.[3] It is estimated that of the $100 billion in care the uninsured use per year, 26% was paid out-of-pocket by the uninsured, or $26 billion. As Uwe Reinhardt wrote, "If the purpose of public policy in this area were to protect American families from financial distress, then presumably some of this out-of-pocket spending by the uninsured would be shifted from the uninsured to the government's budget."[4] The cost of covering these out-of-pocket costs would depend on the generosity of the benefits offered to the uninsured.

- The cost of covering uncompensated care costs provided by hospitals, physicians, and other providers to the uninsured: Currently, $34.5 billion a year is spent on uncompensated care costs, which includes free care, discounted care, and "bad debt" that is written off by the provider if the uninsured person cannot pay.[3] A system that covered the uninsured would likely cover some or all of these uncompensated costs; the exact amount would depend on the specific solution in question.

- Finally, depending on the solution chosen, those who are currently privately insured may also use more health care (e.g. if health care were made available for all with no or minimal cost-sharing, there might be increased usage of health care across the board). Furthermore, there is the possibility that covering the uninsured through a public insurance program may tempt employers to drop coverage and push their employees onto the public insurance program ("crowd-out"); the exact magnitude of this additional cost would depend on the solution chosen.[4]

In summary, the cost of universal health care would be at least $34-$69 billion, plus whatever costs are associated with covering out-of-pocket expenses and uncompensated care for the uninsured. Specific solutions may entail additional expenses as well, depending on their design parameters.

What Are the Costs of Not Achieving Universal Health Care?
In a landmark six-part series on the uninsured, the Institute of Medicine compiled an extensive report on the "hidden" costs of uninsurance.[3]

- Fewer years of participation in the workforce: The annual cost of diminished health and shorter life spans of Americans without insurance is $65-$130 billion. People who do not live as long do not work and contribute to the economy as long.
- Developmental losses for children: children who are uninsured are more likely to suffer delays in development because of poor health, thus affecting their future earning capacity.
- Cost to public programs: Medicare, Social Security Disability Insurance (SSDI), and the criminal justice system have higher costs than they would if there were universal coverage. For Medicare, the reason is that people who are uninsured have poorer health, and this poorer health translates into higher expenses once they become enrolled in Medicare. A similar effect exists for SSDI and the criminal justice system, although to a smaller degree because most people do not end up using these programs whereas the vast majority ultimately enroll in Medicare at age 65.

The Institute of Medicine also studied the cost of high rates of uninsurance to communities.[5]

- Lower health care delivery capacity: Communities with high levels of uninsurance tend to have a lower health care delivery capacity, as providers, burdened by the costs of uncompensated care, reduce staff, relocate, or close.
- Impaired access to emergency departments: Access to ERs is impaired for both uninsured and insured individuals in communities with high rates of uninsurance. The reason is twofold: emergency departments burdened by uncompensated care costs close down or reduce capacity, and uninsured individuals who have nowhere else to turn to for primary care overcrowd ERs.

- Weakened local economy: A high rate of uninsurance and the corresponding burden of uncompensated care costs weaken a community's health infrastructure (e.g. closing or downsizing of local hospitals). Since health care is an important part of a community's economic base, communities suffer economically.
- Adverse effects on public health: Communities with high rates of uninsurance have less effective control of communicable disease (e.g. less vaccinations, less surveillance of TB) and an overall greater disease burden in general. Furthermore, public health agencies may have budgetary problems if the local government has to siphon dollars away to pay for safety net services for the uninsured.

In addition to the costs delineated by the Institute of Medicine, there are several other areas of economic inefficiency because of the lack of universal health care in America:

- Unnecessary use of the ER: the ER is an expensive place to receive care. An average visit to an emergency room costs $383,[6] whereas the average physician's office visit costs $60.[7] It is estimated that 10.7% of ER visits in 2000 were for non-emergencies, costing the system billions of dollars.[8]
- Lack of preventive care and adequate care of chronic diseases: Because the uninsured do not get the preventive and chronic disease care they need, they are more likely to develop complications and advanced stage disease, both of which are expensive to treat. The magnitude of this cost is difficult to estimate, but it is significant.
- "Job lock": Job lock refers to the idea that people stay with their jobs when they would rather work elsewhere because their current job offers health insurance. For example, many individuals opt to stay with their job instead of starting their own business because they are unsure of whether they can get health insurance on the individual market, which has higher premiums and often denies people with

pre-existing conditions. Although the number of people who would be self-employed if there were universal health care is controversial, one study from 2001 put the number at 3.8 million Americans.[9] This loss of entrepreneurship is a real economic cost in a society that is relying on start-ups to offset the loss of jobs that are moving offshore.

The above are the costs of not achieving universal health care in America by any solution. There is a specific subset of costs that would remain if the solution chosen to achieve universal health care builds on the current system of employer-based insurance (e.g. if the solution is not a comprehensive reform that moves to a centralized insurance scheme, like single payer or social insurance).

- Strain on businesses: The employer-based insurance system in America constitutes a tremendous drain on businesses, as skyrocketing health insurance premiums dig further into profit margins and undermine the ability of businesses to invest in expansion. Health insurance premiums in 2005 grew approximately 2-3 times the rate of overall inflation (3.5%) and wage increases (2.7%).[1]
- Loss of global competitiveness: Health insurance costs are built into the prices of American products. Because businesses in other industrialized countries are not responsible for shouldering most of the costs of employee health insurance, American companies are at a competitive disadvantage globally. General Motors reports that every car it makes is $1,500 more expensive because of health care costs, far more than what Japanese and German automakers have to pay.[10]

Do the Costs of Achieving Universal Health Care Outweigh the Benefits?

In 2005, the Emory economist Dr. Kenneth Thorpe published an important report for the National Coalition for Health Care, a strictly non-partisan, broad-based coalition of businesses, providers, unions, and other groups interested in improving the health care system. In this report, Dr. Thorpe calculated the costs to the government of instituting health care for all under four different scenarios:

- Institute an employer mandate plus individual mandate (requiring employers to provide a certain level of health benefits and requiring individuals who do not get employer-based insurance to obtain health insurance through some mechanism);
- Expand public programs such as Medicaid;
- Create a new program for the uninsured modeled after the Federal Employee Health Benefits Plan (FEHBP), the insurance plan for federal employees;
- Create a universal, public financed plan.

This study did not just focus on expanding access; it also assumed significant systemic changes including administrative simplification, computerized physician order entry, an automated patient safety/error reporting system, reduction in inappropriate clinical practice variation, and controls of provider payments and premiums to reach target goals in expenditure growth. According to Thorpe's analysis, each of these four options would save money over 10 years. The first two options would save $320.5 billion over 10 years, the third option would save $369.8 billion over 10 years, and the fourth option would save $1.1 trillion over 10 years.[11]

The important point to take away from Thorpe's study is that universal health care, coupled with cost controls, can save money while expanding health care access to everyone. If universal health care simply expanded access, the net expenditure would be large. The only way to pay for this expanded access is to institute cost controls such as administrative simplification.

Note that it is much easier in some universal health care solutions to institute cost controls than others. For instance, a single payer system allows for a more dramatic reduction of administrative costs than do the other three solutions, all of which build on the current system.

Conclusion

There are real economic costs associated with uninsurance, as detailed above. Although many of these costs are not quantifiable given present data, the idea that universal health care would entail a massive outlay of money with no return does not take into account the hidden economic gains associated with having a healthier and longer living workforce.

Even if one were to assume that universal health care would entail a large outlay of money with no economic return, the amount of money it costs to cover all is literally a drop in the bucket of the US economy. In the end, universal health care is a matter of budgetary priorities and therefore of moral priorities. As the world-famous Princeton health economist Uwe Reinhardt put it, "The issue of universal coverage is not a matter of economics. Little more than 1% of GDP assigned to health could cover all. It is a matter of soul."

[...]

References

1. Kaiser Family Foundation. "Employer Health Benefits 2005 Annual Survey," 2005.

2. Kaiser Family Foundation. "Medicaid: A Primer," 2005.

3. Institute of Medicine. "Hidden Costs: Value Lost," 2002.

4. Reinhardt, U. "Is there Hope for the Uninsured?" Health Affairs Web Exclusive, August 27, 2003.

5. Institute of Medicine. "A Shared Destiny: Community Effects of Uninsurance," 2002.

6. New England Journal of Medicine, "The Costs of Visits to Emergency Departments," 1996.

7. American Medical Association, "Physician Socioeconomic Statistics," 2001.

8. National Center for Health Statistics, "National Hospital Ambulatory Medical Survey: 2000," April 2002.

9. Hopkins, J. "Health insurance costs dog would-be entrepreneurs." USA Today, August 8, 2005.

10. Associated Press. "GM to slash jobs, close more plants." Available at http://www.msnbc.msn.com/id/8129876/from/RL.2/, accessed December 2005.

11. Thorpe, K. "Impacts of Health Care Reform: Projections of Costs and Savings," 2005.

Medical Plutocrats Control the US Health Care System

Robert Kuttner

Robert Kuttner is cofounder and coeditor of the American Prospect. *He is a professor at Brandeis University's Heller School.*

US health care expenditures rose 6.7% in 2006, the government recently reported. According to the Centers for Medicare and Medicaid Services, total health care expenditures exceeded $2.1 trillion, or more than $7,000 for every American man, woman, and child.[1] Medicare costs jumped a record 18.7%, driven by the new privatized drug benefit. Total health care spending, now amounting to 16% of the gross domestic product, is projected to reach 20% in just 7 years.

Relentless medical inflation has been attributed to many factors—the aging population, the proliferation of new technologies, poor diet and lack of exercise, the tendency of supply (physicians, hospitals, tests, pharmaceuticals, medical devices, and novel treatments) to generate its own demand, excessive litigation and defensive medicine, and tax-favored insurance coverage.

Here is a second opinion. Changing demographics and medical technology pose a cost challenge for every nation's system, but ours is the outlier. The extreme failure of the United States to contain medical costs results primarily from our unique, pervasive commercialization. The dominance of for-profit insurance and pharmaceutical companies, a new wave of investor-owned specialty hospitals, and profit-maximizing behavior even by nonprofit players raise costs and distort resource allocation. Profits, billing, marketing, and the gratuitous costs of private bureaucracies siphon off $400 billion to $500 billion of the $2.1 trillion spent, but the more serious and less appreciated

"Market-Based Failure—A Second Opinion on U.S. Health Care Costs," by Robert Kuttner, Massachusetts Medical Society, February 7, 2008. Reprinted by permission.

syndrome is the set of perverse incentives produced by commercial dominance of the system.

Markets are said to optimize efficiencies. But despite widespread belief that competition is the key to cost containment, medicine—with its third-party payers and its partly social mission—does not lend itself to market discipline. Why not?

The private insurance system's main techniques for holding down costs are practicing risk selection, limiting the services covered, constraining payments to providers, and shifting costs to patients. But given the system's fragmentation and perverse incentives, much cost-effective care is squeezed out, resources are increasingly allocated in response to profit opportunities rather than medical need, many attainable efficiencies are not achieved, unnecessary medical care is provided for profit, administrative expenses are high, and enormous sums are squandered in efforts to game the system. The result is a blend of overtreatment and undertreatment—and escalating costs. Researchers calculate that between one fifth and one third of medical outlays do nothing to improve health.

Great health improvements can be achieved through basic public health measures and a population-based approach to wellness and medical care. But entrepreneurs do not prosper by providing these services, and those who need them most are the least likely to have insurance. Innumerable studies have shown that consistent application of standard protocols for conditions such as diabetes, asthma, and elevated cholesterol levels, use of clinically proven screenings such as annual mammograms, provision of childhood immunizations, and changes to diet and exercise can improve health and prevent larger outlays later on. Comprehensive, government-organized, universal health insurance systems are far better equipped to realize these efficiencies because everyone is covered and there are no incentives to pursue the most profitable treatments rather than those dictated by medical need. Although the populations of most countries that belong to the Organization for Economic Cooperation and Development are older than the

US population, these countries have been far more successful at containing costs without compromising care.

Many US insurers do reward physicians for following standard clinical practices, but these incentives do not aggregate to an efficient national system of care. After more than three decades of managed care—and the same three decades of studies by Wennberg and colleagues identifying wide variations in practice patterns—consistent practices are still far from the norm.[2] Commercial incentives are not fixing what's broken.

Instead, cost-containment efforts have fallen heavily on primary care physicians, who have seen caseloads increase and net earnings stagnate or decline. A popular strategy among cost-containment consultants relies on the psychology of income targeting. The idea is that physicians have a mental picture of expected earnings—an income target. If the insurance plan squeezes their income by reducing payments per visit, doctors compensate by increasing their caseload and spending less time with each patient.

This false economy is a telling example of the myopia of commercialized managed care. It may save the plan money in the short run, but as any practicing physician can testify, the strategy has multiple self-defeating effects. A doctor's most precious commodity is time—adequate time to review a chart, take a history, truly listen to a patient. You can't do all that in 10 minutes. Harried primary care doctors are more likely to miss cues, make mistakes, and—ironically enough—order more tests to compensate for lack of hands-on assessment. They are also more likely to make more referrals to specialists for procedures they could perform more cost-effectively themselves, given adequate time and compensation. And the gap between generalist and specialist pay is widening.[3]

A second cost-containment tactic is to hike deductibles and copayments, whose frank purpose is to dissuade people from going to the doctor. But sometimes seeing the doctor is medically indicated, and waiting until conditions are dire costs the system far more money than it saves. Moreover, at some point during each year, more than 80 million Americans go without coverage, which makes them even less likely to seek preventive care.[4]

The system also has inflationary effects on hospitals' revenue-maximization strategies. Large hospitals, which still have substantial bargaining power with insurers, necessarily cross-subsidize services. The emergency department may lose money, but cardiology makes a bundle. So hospitals fiercely defend their profit centers, investing heavily in facilities for lucrative procedures that will attract physicians and patients. For the system as a whole, it would be far more cost-effective to shift resources from subspecialists to primary care. But in an uncoordinated, commercialized system, specialists might take their business elsewhere, so they have the leverage to maintain their incomes and privileges—and thereby distort cost-effective resource allocation.

Defenders of commercialized health care contend that economic incentives work. And indeed they do—but often in perverse ways. The privately regulated medical market is signaling pressured physicians to behave more like entrepreneurs, inspiring some to defect to "boutique medicine," in which well-to-do patients pay a premium, physicians maintain good incomes, and both get leisurely consultation time. It's a convenient solution, but only for the very affluent and their doctors, and it increases overall medical outlays.

Other doctors opt out by becoming proprietors of specialty hospitals, usually day surgeries. In principle, it is cost-effective to shift many procedures to outpatient settings that are less expensive but still offer high-quality care. In a government-organized universal system, the cost savings can be usefully redirected elsewhere. But in our system, the savings go into the surgeons' pockets, and their day hospitals often have a parasitic relationship with community hospitals, which retain the hardest cases and give up the remunerative procedures needed to subsidize those which lose money.

A comprehensive national system is far better positioned to match resources with needs—and not through the so-called rationing of care. (It is the US system that has the most de facto rationing—high rates of uninsurance, exclusions for preexisting conditions, excessive deductibles and copayments, and shorter hospital stays and physician visits.) A universal system suffers far less of the feast-or-famine misallocation of resources driven by profit maximization. It also saves huge sums that our system wastes on administration, billing, marketing, profit, executive compensation, and risk selection. When the British National Health Service faced a shortage of primary care doctors, it adjusted pay schedules and added incentives for high-quality care, and the shortage diminished. Our commercialized system seems incapable of producing that result.

Despite our crisis of escalating costs, dwindling insurance coverage, and deteriorating conditions of medical practice, true national health insurance that would not rely on private insurers remains at the fringes of the national debate. This reality reflects the immense power of the insurance and pharmaceutical industries, the political fragmentation and ambivalence of the medical profession, the intimidation of politicians, and the erroneous media images of dissatisfied patients in universal systems.[5]

Sometimes, we Americans do the right thing only after having exhausted all other alternatives. It remains to be seen how much exhaustion the health care system will suffer before we turn to national health insurance.

References

1. Catlin A, Cowan C, Hartman M, Heffler S. National health spending in 2006: a year of change for prescription drugs. Health Aff (Millwood) 2008;27:14-29

2. Wennberg JE, Gittlesohn A. Small area variations in health care delivery. Science 1973;182:1102-1108

3. 2007 Medical Group Compensation and Financial Survey. Alexandria, VA: American Medical Group Association, 2007.

4. Going without health insurance: nearly one in three non-elderly Americans. Princeton, NJ: Robert Wood Johnson Foundation, March 2003.

5. Schoen C, Osborn R, Doty MM, Bishop M, Peugh J, Murukutla N. Toward higher-performance health systems: adults' health care experiences in seven countries, 2007. Health Aff (Millwood)2007;26:w717-w734

Learning from Diabetes: Why Smart Government Spending Matters

Niranjan Konduri

Niranjan Konduri is a principal technical advisor at Systems for Improved Access to Pharmaceuticals and Services (SIAPS) Program, a US Agency for International Development (USAID)-funded program led by Management Sciences for Health (MSH).

The World Health Organization's first global report on diabetes released this month highlights the disease's "alarming surge" with rates that have quadrupled in fewer than three decades. The report reminds us that essential diabetes medicines and health technologies, including lifesaving insulin, are available in only one in three of the world's poorest countries.

Availability of medicines is certainly an important piece of the complex challenge of ensuring that health systems seamlessly integrate prevention, screening, referral, treatment, and adherence. However, choosing the best way to spend limited public health budgets amid competing priorities is equally important.

Families in low- and middle-income countries can be saddled by out-of-pocket spending on medicines and catastrophic health expenditures. However, on a larger scale, hospitals and even nations can be similarly burdened—and insulin is a major contributor, in part due to its high price. For example, one of Tanzania's district hospitals could spend half its budget on insulin, leaving the other half to cover medicines for 90 percent of remaining diseases. This presents a tough dilemma: Should the district hospital deny treatment to the majority in order to cover the handful that needs insulin?

Likewise, in Ukraine, an analysis by the US Agency for

"Learning from Diabetes: Why Smart Government Spending Matters for SDG Medicines Target," by Niranjan Konduri, Management Sciences for Health, April 21, 2016. Reprinted by permission.

International Development's Systems for Improved Access to Pharmaceuticals and Services Program (USAID SIAPS) found that insulins and analogues accounted for a whopping 15 percent of the total public spending on all medicines procured for the entire nation. This level of spending was consistent across 2013, 2014, and 2015. The total expenditure of 697 million Ukraine hryvnias (USD $31.8 million) in 2015 was 55 percent more than in 2013, due in part to of the sharp decline in the value of the currency.

By contrast, the comparatively wealthy United Kingdom was concerned that its National Health Service could be bankrupted because spending on diabetes medicines had reached 10 percent of its total pharmaceutical budget. Clearly, other countries in a similar situation such as Venezuela may realize that this is not financially sustainable.

Timely Prevention and Efficient Use of Resources

WHO's report strongly makes the case for low- and middle-income countries to focus on diabetes prevention, while ensuring access to medicines and health technologies for those in need. By targeting those at high risk with prevention efforts and identifying patients earlier and managing their diabetes better, countries can conserve their limited medicine budgets.

While countries march toward universal health coverage, medicines benefit programs within health insurance schemes must include an appropriate selection of medicines and health technologies. If countries procured cost-effective human insulin instead of the new-generation analogues, projected annual savings would range from $48,000 to $49 million. In South Africa, for example, analogue insulins are not recommended in their national guidelines and not procured for the public sector.

Health Technology Assessment for Universal Health Coverage

These scenarios force national authorities to grapple with tough decisions on choosing which medicines and health technologies offer the most in terms of health need, population coverage, and value for money.

According to the WHO, "health technology assessment is a systematic approach to evaluate the properties, effects, and impacts of health technologies or interventions. It can be applied to medical devices, medicines, vaccines, procedures, health services, and public health interventions."

To support universal health coverage, the WHO issued a resolution on health technology assessment noting the limited capacity in countries to use resources efficiently. Health technology assessment processes are expected to promote fairness, equity, and transparency for decision-making.

For example, the USAID SIAPS program has supported authorities in South Africa through data-driven analysis to limit the use of expensive insulin pens to children and visually impaired patients. Through various institutional and individual capacity building initiatives, we are working with various stakeholders to manage resources efficiently. Our program helped authorities in the Dominican Republic use an evidence-based selection algorithm to free up nearly $62 million for other priority medicines.

How to Ensure Smarter Government Spending? Here Are 4 Ideas That—Among Many Other Evidence-Based Strategies—Could Help

1. Establish or upgrade reliable tracking systems for medicines spending data. Without good data, it can be hard to identify expenditure trends and use it for decision-making.
2. Ensure that a country's national essential medicines list is periodically updated and reflects public health priorities.
3. Limit public sector procurement and, where applicable, social insurance schemes to the national essential medicines list (or preferred formulary list) to prioritize public spending.

4. Utilize and communicate to the public, a sound national medicines policy as the key political framework for the government to ensure access to efficacious, safe, quality-assured and affordable medicines that are rationally used.

Governments should not have to "break the bank" while aspiring to achieve Sustainable Development Goal (SDG) 3.8 on ensuring access to quality-assured and affordable essential medicines and vaccines for all. As we have seen with diabetes, countries could better use their finite resources on both prevention and the selection of the most appropriate medicines by making health technology assessment a standard way to do business.

CHAPTER 3

Is the Government Responsible for Health Care?

Experts Debate Whether Health Care Is a Federal Responsibility

Julie Rovner

Julie Rovner is a health policy correspondent for NPR specializing in the politics of health care.

I t's a debate that has raged on and off in the United States for more than a century now, with no clear resolution in sight: whether to guarantee health care for every American.

During the past 100 years, medicine has advanced from a rudimentary craft to a scientific pursuit capable of near miracles. Its cost has increased accordingly: In 2006, US health care spending hit $2.1 trillion, or roughly $7,026 for every man, woman and child in the nation.

As a percentage of the gross domestic product, that is substantially more than any other country. Yet a substantial portion of the American population—47 million that same year—lacked any health insurance, according to the US Census Bureau.

As the number of people without insurance increased, so did concern over the problem. But Americans have never neared consensus about what role government in general, and the federal government in particular, should play in ensuring health coverage for all, despite the fact that every other industrialized country has long since established some system of universal insurance.

The stage appears set for yet another major national health insurance debate in 2009, so the Intelligence Squared US series decided to get a head start by choosing it as the topic for its first event of the season. The organization sponsors Oxford-style debates featuring six experts—three on each side—who try to sway an audience that votes before and after the session.

The debate statement was "Universal health coverage should be the federal government's responsibility."

Two of the panelists were Canadian, but they presented sharply divergent views of that country's experience with government-guaranteed health care.

At the start of the event, held at New York's Rockefeller University and moderated by John Donvan of ABC News, 49 percent of the audience agreed with the motion that the government is responsible, 24 percent disagreed and 27 percent said they were undecided.

After the debate, the undecideds split almost equally. Fifty-eight percent of the audience agreed with the motion (a gain of 9 percentage points), 34 percent disagreed (a gain of 10 percentage points), and 8 percent remained undecided.

Highlights from the debate:

For the Motion

Art Kellermann, *a professor of emergency medicine and associate dean for health policy at Emory University, says:* "If everybody practiced medicine as efficiently as they do in Rochester, Minnesota, and Salt Lake City, Utah, Medicare could pay 30 percent less to doctors and hospitals and everybody would get better care. But it won't happen on its own because one person's waste is another person's revenue stream. That's why we need a cop on the beat, and the only cop with the clout to get the health care industry to play by the rules is the federal government."

Paul Krugman, *a professor of economics at Princeton University and a columnist for The New York Times, says:* "The fact of the matter is that our health care system is wildly inefficient, largely because we have an insurance industry that devotes enormous resources to try to identify who really needs health insurance, so as not to give it to them. And we have health care providers devoting enormous resources, fighting with the insurance companies to actually get paid. ... It would be cheaper by far to just cover everybody. We pay this huge price because we've managed to convince ourselves or be convinced that somehow, something that every other advanced country does, and that we do ourselves for the elderly, is impossible."

Michael Rachlis, *a doctor and health policy analyst and a professor at the University of Toronto*, says: "In Toronto right now, because of public response to the concerns about waiting lists, if you need cataract surgery, if you need your knee replaced, if you need a hip replaced, phone one number. You can be seen in an assessment clinic within one week usually, and you can get your surgery within a month after that. And it doesn't cost you any money directly because you pay it in your taxes, and the taxes in Canada as a share of GDP are almost as low as they are in the United States."

Against the Motion

Michael F. Cannon, *the Cato Institute's director of health policy studies*, says: "You can have a health care sector that guarantees universal coverage, or you can have a health care sector that continuously makes medical care better, cheaper and safer, making it easier to deliver on that moral obligation that we have to help the less fortunate among us. You cannot have both."

Sally C. Pipes, *president and CEO of the Pacific Research Institute*, says: "As my friend in Vancouver, Dr. Brian Day, orthopedic surgeon and head of the Canadian Medical Association, told *The New York Times*, Canada is a country in which your dog can get a hip replacement in under a week and in which humans wait two to three years. Is this the kind of government-run health care system Americans desire?"

John Stossel, *an ABC News correspondent and co-anchor of 20/20*, says: "When everything is free, when the government pays for it, everybody wants everything. But the government doesn't have infinite money, so the government then must ration. And they do it by not giving you the latest, most expensive stuff or they make you wait in line."

More Americans Say Government Should Ensure Health Care Coverage

Kristen Bialik

Kristen Bialik is a research assistant at the Pew Research Center.

As the debate continues over repeal of the Affordable Care Act and what might replace it, a growing share of Americans believe that the federal government has a responsibility to make sure all Americans have health care coverage, according to a new Pew Research Center survey.

Currently, 60% of Americans say the government should be responsible for ensuring health care coverage for all Americans, compared with 38% who say this should not be the government's responsibility. The share saying it is the government's responsibility has increased from 51% last year and now stands at its highest point in nearly a decade.

Just as there are wide differences between Republicans and Democrats about the 2010 health care law, the survey also finds partisan differences in views on whether it's the government's responsibility to make sure all Americans have health care coverage. More than eight-in-ten Democrats and Democratic-leaning independents (85%) say the federal government should be responsible for health care coverage, compared with just 32% of Republicans and Republican leaners.

The survey also finds continued differences on this question by race and ethnicity as well as income. A large majority of blacks and Hispanics (85% and 84%, respectively) say the government should be responsible for coverage, while non-Hispanic whites are split on the issue (49% agree, 49% disagree). And while about three-quarters of those with family incomes of less than $30,000 per year (74%) say the government should ensure coverage, only about half (53%) of those with incomes of $75,000 or higher say the same.

The belief that the government has a responsibility to ensure health coverage has increased across many groups over the past year, but the rise has been particularly striking among lower- and middle-income Republicans.

Currently, 52% of Republicans with family incomes below $30,000 say the federal government has a responsibility to ensure health coverage for all, up from just 31% last year. There also has been a 20-percentage-point increase among Republicans with incomes of $30,000-$74,999 (34% now, 14% last year). But there has been no significant change among those with incomes of $75,000 or more (18% now, 16% then).

Those who think government should ensure health coverage for all are divided on a follow-up question about whether health insurance should be provided through a mix of private insurance companies and the government (29% of the overall public) or if the government alone should provide insurance (28% of the public).

Overall, 43% of Democrats and Democratic leaners support a so-called single payer approach, but this approach is more popular among liberal Democrats (51%) than among conservative and moderate Democrats (38%).

Most of those on the other side of the issue—people who say the government does *not* have a responsibility to ensure health coverage—say on a subsequent question that the government should continue Medicare and Medicaid (32% of the overall public), while just 5% of the public says the government should have no role in health care.

Among Republicans and Republican leaners, most of whom (67%) say the government does not have a responsibility for ensuring health coverage, there is very little support for the government not being involved in health care at all. Just 10% of Republicans favor no government involvement, while 56% say it should continue Medicare and Medicaid.

While Republicans in Congress have already taken the first steps toward repealing the ACA, Americans remain largely divided on what Congress should do with the health care law. Overall, in a Pew Research Center survey in December, 39% said it should be repealed, while an equal share (39%) said the law should be expanded. Just 15% of Americans said the law should be left as is. Although the public is divided on the future of the law, there is bipartisan support for a number of ACA provisions. Regardless of their personal views of the law, a small majority (53%) expects its major provisions will likely be eliminated.

A December Kaiser Family Foundation survey shows repealing the law is not the public's top health care priority for President-elect Donald Trump and the next Congress. Lowering the amount individuals pay for health care tops the list, with 67% of Americans saying it should be a top priority for the next administration. This is followed by lowering the cost of prescription drugs (61%) and dealing with the prescription-painkiller addiction epidemic (45%). Only 37% of the public says repealing the law should be the administration's top priority, though views differ widely by party.

The French Health Care System: Low Costs, Great Care

Isabelle Durand-Zaleski

Isabelle Durand-Zaleski (MD, PhD) is a professor of public health.

What Is the Role of the Government?

The provision of health care in France is a national responsibility. The Ministry of Social Affairs, Health, and Women's Rights is responsible for defining national strategy. Over the past two decades, the state has been increasingly involved in controlling health expenditures funded by statutory health insurance (SHI).[1]

Planning and regulation within health care involve negotiations among provider representatives, the state, and SHI. Outcomes of these negotiations are translated into laws passed by Parliament.

In addition to setting national strategy, the responsibilities of the central government include allocating budgeted expenditures among different sectors (hospitals, ambulatory care, mental health, and services for disabled residents) and, with respect to hospitals, among regions. The ministry is represented in the regions by the regional health agencies, which are responsible for population health and health care, including prevention and care delivery, public health, and social care. Health and social care for elderly and disabled people come under the jurisdiction of the General Councils, which are the governing bodies at the local (departmental) level.

Who Is Covered and How Is Insurance Financed?

Publicly Financed Health Insurance

Total health expenditures constituted 12 percent of GDP (EUR257 billion, or USD310 billion) in 2014, of which 76.6 percent was publicly financed.

SHI is financed by employer and employee payroll taxes (50%); a national earmarked income tax (35%); taxes levied on tobacco

"The French Health Care System," by Isabelle Durand-Zaleski, in International Profiles of Health Care Systems 2017, The Commonwealth Fund. Reprinted by permission.

and alcohol, the pharmaceutical industry, and voluntary health insurance companies (13%); and state subsidies (2%).

Coverage is universal and compulsory, provided to all residents by noncompetitive SHI. As of January 2016, SHI eligibility is universally granted under the PUMA (Protection universelle maladie, or universal health care coverage) law.[2] Citizens can opt out of SHI only in rare cases—for example, individuals employed by foreign companies.

The state finances health services for undocumented immigrants who have applied for residence. Visitors from elsewhere in the European Union (EU) are covered by an EU insurance card. Non-EU visitors are covered for emergency care only.

Private Health Insurance

Most voluntary health insurance (VHI) is complementary, covering mainly the copayments for usual care, balance billing, and vision and dental care (minimally covered by SHI). Complementary insurance is provided mainly by not-for-profit, employment-based mutual associations or provident institutions, which are allowed to cover only copayments for care provided under SHI; 95 percent of the population is covered either through employers or via means-tested vouchers. Private for-profit companies offer both supplementary and complementary health insurance, but only for a limited list of services.

VHI finances 13.5 percent of total health expenditure.[3] The extent of VHI coverage varies widely, but all VHI contracts cover the difference between the SHI reimbursement rate and the service fee according to the official fee schedule. Coverage of balance billing is also commonly offered, and most contracts cover the balance for services billed at up to 300 percent of the official fee.

In 2013, standards for employer-sponsored VHI were established by law to reduce inequities in coverage stemming from variations in access and quality. By 2017, all employees will benefit from employer-sponsored insurance (for which they pay 50% of the cost), which will cover at least 125 percent of SHI fees for dental care and EUR100 (USD121) for vision care per year.[4] The population of beneficiaries without supplementary insurance is estimated at 4 million. Choice among insurance plans is determined by the industry in which the employer operates.

What Is Covered?

Services

Lists of procedures, drugs, and medical devices covered under SHI are defined at the national level and apply to all regions of the country. The health ministry, a pricing committee within the ministry, and SHI funds set these lists, rates of coverage, and prices.

SHI covers hospital care and treatment in public or private rehabilitation or physiotherapy institutions; outpatient care provided by general practitioners, specialists, dentists, and midwives; diagnostic services prescribed by doctors and carried out by laboratories and paramedical professionals; prescription drugs, medical appliances, and prostheses that have been approved for reimbursement; and prescribed health care–related transportation and home care. It also partially covers long-term hospice and mental health care and provides only minimal coverage of outpatient vision and dental care.

While preventive services in general receive limited coverage, there is full reimbursement for targeted services, such as immunization, mammography, and colorectal cancer screening, as well as targeted populations. A measure of the "Touraine law," adopted on April 14, 2015, mandated the legalization of drug-use centers over a subsequent six-year period. These centers will be used exclusively for treatment of especially vulnerable drug addicts, under the supervision of health professionals.[5]

Cost-Sharing and Out-of-Pocket Spending

Cost-sharing takes three forms: coinsurance; copayments (the portion of fees not covered by SHI); and balance billing in primary and specialist care. In 2014, total out-of-pocket spending made up 8.5 percent of total health expenditures (excluding the portion covered by supplementary insurance), a lower percentage than in previous years—possibly because of the agreement signed between physicians' unions and government to limit balance billing in exchange for its voluntary capping at twice the official fee. This contract offers patients partial reimbursement of balance billing by SHI and reduced social charges for physicians.

Most out-of-pocket spending is for dental and vision services, for which official fees are very low, not more than a few euros for glasses or hearing aids and a maximum of EUR200 (USD241) for dentures, but all of these are commonly balance-billed at more than 10 times the official fee. The share of out-of-pocket spending on dental and optical services is decreasing, however. At the same time, out-of-pocket expenditures on drugs are increasing, owing to increased VHI coverage of dental and optical care and increasing numbers of delisted drugs, as well as a rise in self-medication.

Coinsurance rates are applied to all health services and drugs listed in the benefit package and vary by:

- type of care (inpatient, 20%; doctor visits, 30%; and dental, 30%)
- the effectiveness of prescription drugs (highly effective drugs, like insulin, carry no coinsurance; rates for all other drugs are 15% to 100%, depending on therapeutic value)
- compliance with the recently implemented gatekeeping system

Safety Net

People with low incomes are entitled to free or state-sponsored VHI, free vision care, and free dental care, with the total number of such beneficiaries estimated at around 10 percent of the population.[6] Exemptions from coinsurance apply to individuals with any of 32 specified chronic illnesses (13% of the population, with exemption limited to treatment for those conditions); individuals who benefit from either complete state-sponsored medical coverage (3%) or means-tested vouchers for complementary health insurance (6%); and individuals receiving invalidity and work-injury benefits (2%).[7] Hospital coinsurance applies only to the first 31 days in hospital, and some surgical interventions are exempt. Children and people with low incomes are exempt from paying nonreimbursable copayments.

How Is the Delivery System Organized and Financed?

Collective agreements between representatives of the health professions and SHI, signed at the national level, apply to all but those professionals who expressly opt out. These agreements set the fee schedule as well as coordination and quality incentives.

[...]

What Are the Key Entities for Health System Governance?

The health ministry sets and implements government policy in the areas of public health and the organization and financing of the health care system, within the framework of the Public Health Act. It regulates roughly 75 percent of health care expenditure on the basis of the overall framework established by Parliament, which includes a shared responsibility with statutory health insurers for defining the benefit package, setting prices and provider fees (including DRG fees and copayments), and pricing drugs.

The French Health Products Safety Agency oversees the safety of health products, from manufacturing to marketing. The agency also coordinates vigilance activities relating to all relevant products.

The Agency for Information on Hospital Care manages the information systematically collected from all hospital admissions and used for hospital planning and financing.

The remit of the National Agency for the Quality Assessment of Health and Social Care Organizations encompasses the promotion of patient rights and the development of preventive measures to avoid mistreatment, particularly in vulnerable populations such as the elderly and disabled, children, adolescents, and socially marginalized people. It produces practice guidelines for the health and social care sector and evaluates organizations and services.

The National Health Authority (HAS) is the main health technology assessment body, with in-house expertise as well as the authority to commission assessments from external groups. The HAS remit is diverse, ranging from the assessment of drugs, medical devices, and procedures to publication of guidelines, accreditation of health care organizations, and certification of doctors.

Competition is limited to VHI, whose providers are supervised by the Mutual Insurance Funds Control Authority.

The Public Health Agency (*Santé publique France*) was created in 2016 to protect population health.

What Are the Major Strategies to Ensure Quality of Care?

National plans have been developed for treatment of rare diseases and a number of chronic conditions, including cancer and Alzheimer's, and rare diseases, as well as for prevention and healthy aging. These plans establish governance (for example, the cancer plan to coordinate research and treatment in cancer and establish guidelines for medical practice and activity thresholds), develop tools, and coordinate existing organizations. All plans emphasize the importance of supporting caregivers and ensuring patients' quality of life, in addition to enforcing compliance with guidelines and promoting evidence-based practice.

The HAS publishes an evidence-based basic benefit package for 32 chronic conditions. Further guidance on recommended care pathways covers chronic obstructive pulmonary disease, heart failure, Parkinson's, and end-stage renal disease.

SHI and the health ministry fund "provider networks" in which participating professionals share guidelines and protocols, agree on best practices, and have access to a common patient record. Regional authorities fund telemedicine pilot programs to improve care coordination and access to care for specific conditions or populations, like newborns or the elderly. The Paerpa (*Personnes agées en risque de perte d'autonomie*) program, established in 2014 in nine pilot regions, is a nationwide endeavor to improve the quality of life and coordination of interventions for the frail elderly.

For self-employed physicians, certification and revalidation are organized by an independent body approved by the HAS. For hospital physicians, both can be performed as part of the hospital accreditation process.

Doctors, midwives, nurses, and other professionals must undergo continuous learning activities, which are audited every fourth or fifth year. Optional accreditation exists for a number of high-risk medical specialties, such as obstetrics, surgery, and cardiology. Accredited physicians can claim a deduction on their professional insurance premiums.

Hospitals must be accredited every four years; criteria and accreditation reports are publicly available on the HAS website (www.has-sante.fr). CompaqH, a national program of performance indicators, also reports results on selected indicators. Quality assurance and risk management in hospitals are monitored nationally by the health ministry, which publishes online technical information, data on hospital activity, and data on control of hospital-acquired infections. Currently, financial rewards or penalties are not linked to public reporting, although they remain a contested issue. Information on individual physicians is not available.

What Is Being Done to Reduce Disparities?

There is a 6.3-year gap in life expectancy between males in the highest and males in the lowest social categories[13] and poorer self-reported health among those with state-sponsored insurance and no complementary insurance. The 2004 Public Health Act set targets for reducing inequities in access to care related to geographic availability of services (so far, only nurses have agreed to limit new practices in overserved areas), financial barriers (out-of-pocket payments will be limited by state-sponsored complementary insurance), and inequities in prevention related to obesity, screening, and immunization. In 2009, launching its Second Cancer Plan, France placed inequalities at the heart of its public health policy. In 2012, the French president reaffirmed this priority with the Third Cancer Plan and later the 2015 Touraine law.[14] A contractual agreement allows for the use of incentives for physicians practicing in underserved areas, the extension of third-party payment, and enforced limitations on denial of care.

National surveys showing regional variations in health and access to health care are reported by the health ministry.

What Is Being Done to Promote Delivery System Integration and Care Coordination?

Inadequate coordination in the health care system remains a problem. Various quality-related initiatives piloted by the health ministry or by regional agencies aim to improve the coordination of hospital, out-of-hospital, and social care (see above). They target the elderly and fragile populations and attempt to streamline the health care pathway, integrating providers of health and social care via a shared portal and case managers.

[...]

References

1.   O. Nay, S. Béjean, D. Benamouzig et al., "Achieving Universal Health Coverage in France: Policy Reforms and the Challenge of Inequalities," Lancet, May 28, 2016 387(10034):2236–49.

2.   www.ameli.fr.

3.   DREES, Les dépenses de santé en 2014, Etudes et Résultats, no. 935, Ministère des Affaires sociales et de la Santé, Sept. 15, 2015.

4.   Please note that, throughout this profile, all figures in USD were converted from EUR at a rate of about EUR0.83 per USD, the purchasing power parity conversion rate for GDP in 2014 reported by OECD (2015) for France.

5.   O. Nay, S. Béjean, D. Benamouzig et al., "Achieving Universal Health Coverage in France: Policy Reforms and the Challenge of Inequalities," Lancet, May 28, 2016 387(10034):2236–49.

6.   DREES, Les dépenses de santé en 2014, Etudes et Résultats, no. 935, Ministère des Affaires sociales et de la Santé, Sept. 15, 2015.

7.   www.risquesprofessionnels.ameli.fr

8.   DREES, Portrait des professionnels de santé, Série Etudes et Recherche, no. 134, Ministère des Affaires sociales et de la Santé, Feb. 2016.

9.   Ibid.

10.   Ibid.

11. O. Nay, S. Béjean, D. Benamouzig et al., "Achieving Universal Health Coverage in France: Policy Reforms and the Challenge of Inequalities," Lancet, May 28, 2016 387(10034):2236–49.

12. Cour des Comptes, Le maintien à domicile des personnes âgées en perte d'autonomie, July 2016, www.ccomptes.fr.

13. DREES, Les dépenses de santé en 2014, Etudes et Résultats, no. 935, Ministère des Affaires sociales et de la Santé, Sept. 15, 2015; O. Nay, S. Béjean, D. Benamouzig et al., "Achieving Universal Health Coverage in France: Policy Reforms and the Challenge of Inequalities," Lancet, May 28, 2016 387(10034):2236–49.

14. Nay et al., ibid.

15. Ibid.

16. Dossier Médical Personnel, 2016.

17. CNAMTS, Direction Déléguée des Finances et de la Comptabilité, Comptes CNAMTS exercice 2015.

18. IRDES, Historique de la politique du médicament en France.

Universal Health Care Makes Everyone's Life Better

Kathleen A. Lavidge

Kathleen A. Lavidge is a former vice president of American Express. She has been an active Stanford volunteer for many years, serving as a co-chair for Leading Matters in London, a major gifts and reunion volunteer, and a member of the Parents' Advisory Board.

I have lived in England, which has universal healthcare, for 14 years, and I have become a firm believer in the benefits universal access to healthcare brings to all—even those who do not need or intend to use it.

In the UK, healthcare is a universal right: You will be treated the same way whether you are working for a corporation or are a self-employed dance teacher; whether you are retired, or have just been made redundant. In England, if you need healthcare, you get it—at no cost. There are no forms to fill out and no insurance claims to file or fight over. If the ambulance is called, no one is going to ask to see your health insurance card before they put you in the vehicle, nor will they detour away from the closest hospital to find the one that takes "charity" cases.

In a nutshell, the primary benefit of universal healthcare is that it improves the quality of life for everyone.

- No one in England remains in a job they absolutely hate because they are afraid of losing healthcare insurance for themselves or a family member.
- No one stays in a job because they have a "pre-existing" condition and know they will never be covered again.

"Does universal healthcare make everyone's life better?" by Kathleen A. Lavidge, Yale School of Management, April 23, 2008. Reprinted by permission. This article originally appeared in Q3, a magazine published by the Yale School of Management (insights.som.yale.edu).

- No one has to worry about having to mortgage their house to pay the hospital, doctor, or pharmacy while they are waiting for repayment from the insurance company, which may never come.
- No one has to worry because they have a significant illness and their insurance company has told them they have reached the maximum payout under their policy.
- No one has to become frantic when an uninsured relative gets into an accident, and assets saved for a well-planned retirement are put at risk in order to assure care for the injured individual.
- No one has to fear a true accident occurring on their property and finding out that the lawyers plan to file a big lawsuit because the injured party does not have health insurance.
- No one worries that the last six months of their life will deplete their family's savings, forcing them to choose whether or not to pay for treatments.
- No one worries that parents too young to qualify for Medicare will become a financial burden if they become ill.
- No one has to decide that that lump can wait to be checked or that blood in their stool is not really "too serious"—only to have it truly become too serious.
- No one is frantic when a child is born with a serious, but treatable, defect because there is no insurance to cover the hospitals and doctors.

In the United States today, it is a very lucky family, indeed, that could not relate to one of the possible fears listed above.

What does universal access to healthcare here in England do for me when it eliminates these anxieties? It makes my quality of life significantly more pleasant. One significant "edge" in life goes away. It just does not exist. Each person I come across, every day, whether in person, on the phone, or passing by me in his or her car, I *know* has access to healthcare. *They know* they have access to healthcare. And, the result is a better quality of life *for me*. How does that benefit me? It makes my everyday dealings with people more pleasant, less stressful. Life is fairer … and better.

Today, in America, it feels like the population is divided in two. The division is not the Republicans and the Democrats. It is not the educated and the undereducated. It is not the wealthy and the poor. It is those with access to adequate healthcare and those without it. It generates a "haves and have nots" culture that is more profoundly felt than any ideological division.

Those without access to healthcare live with a level of fear about their futures that cannot even be fathomed by others. Everything is at risk if someone they love becomes seriously hurt or ill. Those without health insurance are America's "second class" citizens, regardless of education, age, gender, race, or religious convictions. They are at the bottom of the totem pole, and they know it.

Imagine taking away those levels of worry in the United States. Imagine knowing that the people who touch your life are going to be cared for: that great kid down the block who just graduated from State U and then finds out he has Hodgkin's lymphoma; or that young man who mows your lawn, who accidentally gets a deep gouge in his leg when he empties the mower into the compost heap; or your daughter's amazing piano teacher who says she is a little worried about a mole that has appeared on her back; or anyone in a world of wonderful, caring people, who today either cannot get or cannot afford healthcare. Life would just be better in that world. You would know that they, like you, are cared for and worthy of receiving care.

My husband and I are planning to return to live in the States in the next year. I am concerned that when I return I will run into the unpleasantness of the "haves and have nots" of healthcare. I don't want to feel that every day someone whose life touches mine may be angry/fearful/scared/frustrated/petrified because they lack access to healthcare.

I am not suggesting how to create universal healthcare access in the United States. That is for the policy experts to figure out. And I am not advocating providing universal discretionary services, such as cosmetic surgery, which do not maintain and save lives. I also acknowledge that America has the best healthcare in the world, for those who can afford it. And, I know the English system is not perfect. For example, it has long queues for non-urgent procedures, like knee replacements. My point is that these are issues of execution.

I am just trying to keep us focused on the real goal: access to healthcare for everyone. Why? Because it will make *everyone's* life better.

The Right to Health for Everyone

Office of the United Nations High Commissioner for Human Rights

The Office of the United Nations High Commissioner for Human Rights (OHCHR) is a United Nations agency that works to promote and protect the human rights that are guaranteed under international law.

[…]

How Does the Right to Health Apply to Specific Groups?

Some groups or individuals, such as children, women, persons with disabilities or persons living with HIV/AIDS, face specific hurdles in relation to the right to health. These can result from biological or socio-economic factors, discrimination and stigma, or, generally, a combination of these. Considering health as a human right requires specific attention to different individuals and groups of individuals in society, in particular those living in vulnerable situations. Similarly, States should adopt positive measures to ensure that specific individuals and groups are not discriminated against. For instance, they should disaggregate their health laws and policies and tailor them to those most in need of assistance rather than passively allowing seemingly neutral laws and policies to benefit mainly the majority groups.

To illustrate what the standards related to the right to health mean in practice, this chapter focuses on the following groups: women, children and adolescents, persons with disabilities, migrants and persons living with HIV/AIDS.

Women

Women are affected by many of the same health conditions as men, but women experience them differently. The prevalence of poverty and economic dependence among women, their experience

"The Right to Health - Fact Sheet No. 31," Office of the United Nations High Commissioner for Human Rights & World Health Organization, 2007. Reprinted by permission.

of violence, gender bias in the health system and society at large, discrimination on the grounds of race or other factors, the limited power many women have over their sexual and reproductive lives and their lack of influence in decision-making are social realities which have an adverse impact on their health. So women face particular health issues and particular forms of discrimination, with some groups, including refugee or internally displaced women, women in slums and suburban settings, indigenous and rural women, women with disabilities or women living with HIV/AIDS, facing multiple forms of discrimination, barriers and marginalization in addition to gender discrimination.

Both the International Covenant on Economic, Social and Cultural Rights and the Convention on the Elimination of All Forms of Discrimination against Women require the elimination of discrimination against women in health care as well as guarantees of equal access for women and men to health-care services. Redressing discrimination in all its forms, including in the provision of health care, and ensuring equality between men and women are fundamental objectives of treating health as a human right. In this respect, the Convention on the Elimination of All Forms of Discrimination against Women (art. 14) specifically calls upon States to ensure that "women in rural areas ... participate in and benefit from rural development" and "have access to adequate health-care facilities, ... counselling and services in family planning."

The Committee on the Elimination of Discrimination against Women further requires States parties to ensure women have appropriate services in connection with pregnancy, childbirth and the post-natal period, including family planning and emergency obstetric care. The requirement for States to ensure safe motherhood and reduce maternal mortality and morbidity is implicit here.

Sexual and reproductive health is also a key aspect of women's right to health. States should enable women to have control over and decide freely and responsibly on matters related to their sexuality, including their sexual and reproductive health, free from coercion, lack of information, discrimination and violence. The Programme of Action of the International Conference on Population and Development[1] and the Beijing Platform for Action[2] highlighted the right of men and women to be informed and to have access to safe, effective, affordable and acceptable methods of family planning of their choice, and the right of access to appropriate health-care services that will enable women to go safely through pregnancy and childbirth and provide couples with the best chance of having a healthy infant.

Children and Adolescents

Children face particular health challenges related to the stage of their physical and mental development, which makes them especially vulnerable to malnutrition and infectious diseases and, when they reach adolescence, to sexual, reproductive and mental health problems.

Most childhood deaths can be attributed to a few major causes—acute respiratory infections, diarrhoea, measles, malaria and malnutrition—or a combination of these. In this regard both the International Covenant on Economic, Social and Cultural Rights and the Convention on the Rights of the Child recognize the obligation on States to reduce infant and child mortality and to combat disease and malnutrition. In addition, a baby who has lost his or her mother to pregnancy and childbirth complications has a higher risk of dying in early childhood. Infants' health is so closely linked to women's reproductive and sexual health that the Convention on the Rights of the Child directs States to ensure access to essential health services for the child and his/her family, including pre- and post-natal care for mothers.

Children are also increasingly at risk because of HIV infections occurring mostly through mother-to-child transmission (a baby born to an HIV-positive mother has a 25 to 35 percent chance of becoming infected during pregnancy, childbirth or breastfeeding). Accordingly, States should take measures to prevent such transmission through, for instance: medical protocols for HIV testing during pregnancy; information campaigns among women on these forms of transmission; the provision of affordable drugs; and the provision of care and treatment to HIV-infected women, their infants and families, including counselling and infant feeding options.

Governments and health professionals should treat all children and adolescents in a non-discriminatory manner. This means that they should pay particular attention to the needs and rights of specific groups, such as children belonging to minorities or indigenous communities, intersex children[3] and, generally, young girls and adolescent girls, who in many contexts are prevented from accessing a wide range of services, including health care. More specifically, girls should have equal access to adequate nutrition, safe environments, and physical and mental health services. Appropriate measures should be taken to abolish harmful traditional practices that affect mostly girls' health, such as female genital mutilation, early marriage, and preferential feeding and care of boys.

Children who have experienced neglect, exploitation, abuse, torture or any other form of cruel, inhuman or degrading treatment or punishment also require specific protection by States. The Convention on the Rights of the Child (art. 39) stresses the responsibility of the State for promoting children's physical and psychological recovery and social reintegration.

While adolescents are in general a healthy population group, they are prone to risky behaviour, sexual violence and sexual exploitation. Adolescent girls are also vulnerable to early and/or unwanted pregnancies. Adolescents' right to health is therefore dependent on health care that respects confidentiality and privacy and includes appropriate mental, sexual and reproductive health services and information. Adolescents are, moreover, particularly vulnerable to sexually transmitted diseases, including HIV/AIDS. In many regions of the world, new HIV infections are heavily concentrated among young people (15–24 years of age).[4] Effective prevention programmes should address sexual health and ensure equal access to HIV-related information and preventive measures such as voluntary counselling and testing and affordable contraceptive methods and services.

[…]

Migrants

Migration has become a major political, social and economic phenomenon, with significant human rights consequences. The International Organization for Migration estimates that, today, there are nearly 200 million international migrants worldwide. According to the International Labour Organization, 90 million of them are migrant workers. Although migration has implications for the right to health in both home and host countries, the focus here is on migrants in host countries. Their enjoyment of the right to health is often limited merely because they are migrants, as well as owing to other factors such as discrimination, language and cultural barriers, or their legal status. While they all face particular problems linked to their specific status and situation (undocumented or irregular migrants and migrants held in detention being particularly at risk),[5] many migrants will face similar obstacles to realizing their human rights, including their right to health.

States have explicitly stated before international human rights bodies or in national legislation that they cannot or do not wish to provide the same level of protection to migrants as to their own citizens. Accordingly, most countries have defined their health obligations towards non-citizens in terms of "essential care" or "emergency health care" only. Since these concepts mean different things in different countries, their interpretation is often left to individual health-care staff. Practices and laws may therefore be discriminatory.

The International Convention on the Protection of the Rights of All Migrant Workers and Members of Their Families (art. 28) stipulates that all migrant workers and their families have the right to emergency medical care for the preservation of their life or the avoidance of irreparable harm to their health. Such care should be provided regardless of any irregularity in their stay or employment. The Convention further protects migrant workers in the workplace and stipulates that they shall enjoy treatment not less favourable than that which applies to nationals of the State of employment in respect of conditions of work, including safety and health (art. 25).

The Committee on the Elimination of Racial Discrimination, in its general recommendation N° 30 (2004) on non-citizens, and the Committee on Economic, Social and Cultural Rights, in its general comment N° 14 (2000) on the right to the highest attainable standard of health, both stress that States parties should respect the right of non-citizens to an adequate standard of physical and mental health by, inter alia, refraining from denying or limiting their access to preventive, curative and palliative health services. The Special Rapporteur on Health has also stressed that sick asylum-seekers or undocumented persons, as some of the most vulnerable persons within a population, should not be denied their human right to medical care.

Finally, migrants' right to health is closely related to and dependent on their working and living conditions and legal status. In order to comprehensively address migrants' health issues, States should also take steps to realize their rights to, among other things, adequate housing, safe and healthy working conditions, an adequate standard of living, food, information, liberty and security of person, due process, and freedom from slavery and compulsory labour.

[...]

Notes

[1] *Report of the International Conference on Population and Development, Cairo, 5–13 September 1994* (United Nations publication, Sales N° E.95.XIII.18).

[2] Beijing Declaration and Platform for Action, *Report of the Fourth World Conference on Women, Beijing, 4–15 September 1995* (United Nations publication, Sales N° E.96.IV.13), chap. I, resolution 1.

[3] Intersex children are born with internal and external sex organs that are neither exclusively male nor exclusively female.

[4] Joint United Nations Programme on HIV/AIDS and World Health Organization, *AIDS epidemic update: December 2006*, p. 9.

[5] Persons granted refugee status or internally displaced persons do not fall into the category of migrants. See "Specific groups and individuals: migrant workers" (E/CN.4/2005/85).

Accountable Care Organizations Help Health Care

Jenny Gold

Jenny Gold is a senior correspondent with Kaiser Health News. She covers the health care industry, the Affordable Care Act, and health care disparities for radio and print publications.

One of the main ways the Affordable Care Act seeks to reduce health care costs is by encouraging doctors, hospitals and other health care providers to form networks that coordinate patient care and become eligible for bonuses when they deliver that care more efficiently.

The law takes a carrot-and-stick approach by encouraging the formation of accountable care organizations (ACOs) in the Medicare program. Providers make more if they keep their patients healthy. About 6 million Medicare beneficiaries are now in an ACO, and, combined with the private sector, at least 744 organizations have become ACOs since 2011. An estimated 23.5 million Americans are now being served by an ACO. You may even be in one and not know it.

While ACOs are touted as a way to help fix an inefficient payment system that rewards more, not better, care, some economists warn they could lead to greater consolidation in the health care industry, which could allow some providers to charge more if they're the only game in town.

ACOs have become one of the most talked about new ideas in Obamacare. Here are answers to some common questions about how they work:

What Is an Accountable Care Organization?

An ACO is a network of doctors and hospitals that shares financial and medical responsibility for providing coordinated care to patients in hopes of limiting unnecessary spending. At the heart of each patient's care is a primary care physician.

In Obamacare, each ACO has to manage the health care needs of a minimum of 5,000 Medicare beneficiaries for at least three years.

Think of it as buying a television, says Harold Miller, president and CEO of the Center for Healthcare Quality & Payment Reform in Pittsburgh, Pa. A TV manufacturer like Sony may contract with many suppliers to build sets. Like Sony does for TVs, Miller says, an ACO brings together the different component parts of care for the patient—primary care, specialists, hospitals, home health care, etc.—and ensures that all of the "parts work well together."

The problem with most health systems today, Miller says, is that patients are getting each part of their health care separately. "People want to buy individual circuit boards, not a whole TV," he says. "If we can show them that the TV works better, maybe they'll buy it," rather than assembling a patchwork of services themselves.

Why Did Congress Include ACOs in the Law?

As lawmakers searched for ways to reduce the national deficit, Medicare became a prime target. With baby boomers entering retirement age, the costs of caring for elderly and disabled Americans are expected to soar.

The health law created the Medicare Shared Savings Program. In it, ACOs make providers jointly accountable for the health of their patients, giving them financial incentives to cooperate and save money by avoiding unnecessary tests and procedures. For ACOs to work, they have to seamlessly share information. Those that save money while also meeting quality targets keep a portion of the savings. Providers can choose to be at risk of losing money if they want to aim for a bigger reward, or they can enter the program with no risk at all.

In addition, the Centers for Medicare & Medicaid Services (CMS) created a second strategy, called the Pioneer Program, for high-performing health systems to pocket more of the expected savings in exchange for taking on greater financial risk.

In 2014, the 20 ACOs in the Medicare Pioneer Program and 333 in the Medicare Shared Savings generated $411 million in total savings but after paying bonuses, the program resulted in a net loss of $2.6 million to the Medicare trust fund. That's far less than 1 percent of Medicare spending during that period.

Still the program is expected to be expanded and Health and Human Services Secretary Sylvia Burwell has set a goal of tying 50 percent of all traditional Medicare payments to quality or value by 2018 through new payment models, including ACOs.

How Are ACOs Paid?

In Medicare's traditional fee-for-service payment system, doctors and hospitals generally are paid for each test and procedure. That drives up costs, experts say, by rewarding providers for doing more, even when it's not needed. ACOs don't do away with fee for service, but they create an incentive to be more efficient by offering bonuses when providers keep costs down. Doctors and hospitals have to meet specific quality benchmarks, focusing on prevention and carefully managing patients with chronic diseases. In other words, providers get paid more for keeping their patients healthy and out of the hospital.

If an ACO is unable to save money, it could be stuck with the costs of investments made to improve care, such as adding new nurse care managers. An ACO also may have to pay a penalty if it doesn't meet performance and savings benchmarks, although few have opted into that program yet. ACOs sponsored by physicians or rural providers, however, can apply to receive payments in advance to help them build the infrastructure necessary for coordinated care—a concession the Obama administration made after complaints from rural hospitals.

In 2014, the third year of the Medicare ACO program, 97 ACOs qualified for shared savings payments of more than $422 million.

How Do ACOs Work for Patients?

Doctors and hospitals will likely refer patients to hospitals and specialists within the ACO network. But patients are usually still free to see doctors of their choice outside the network without paying more. Providers who are part of an ACO are required to alert their patients, who can choose to go to another doctor if they are uncomfortable participating. The patient can decline to have his data shared within the ACO.

Who's in Charge—Hospitals, Doctors or Insurers?

ACOs can include hospitals, specialists, post-acute providers and even private companies like Walgreens. The only must-have element is primary care physicians, who serve as the linchpin of the program.

In private ACOs, insurers can also play a role, though they aren't in charge of medical care. Some regions of the country, including parts of California, already had large multi-specialty physician groups that became ACOs on their own by networking with neighboring hospitals.

In other regions, large hospital systems are scrambling to buy up physician practices with the goal of becoming ACOs that directly employ the majority of their providers. Because hospitals usually have access to capital, they may have an easier time than doctors in financing the initial investment, for instance to create the electronic record system necessary to track patients.

Some of the largest health insurers in the country, including Humana, UnitedHealth and Aetna, have formed their own ACOs for the private market. Insurers say they are essential to the success of an ACO because they track and collect the data on patients that allow systems to evaluate patient care and report on the results.

If I Don't Like HMOs, Why Should I Consider an ACO?

ACOs may sound a lot like health maintenance organizations. "Some people say ACOs are HMOs in drag," says Kelly Devers, a senior fellow at the Urban Institute. But there are some critical differences—notably, an ACO patient is not required to stay in the network.

Steve Lieberman, a consultant and senior adviser to the Health Policy Project at the Bipartisan Policy Center in Washington, DC, explains that ACOs aim to replicate "the performance of an HMO" in holding down the cost of care while avoiding "the structural features that give the HMO control over [patient] referral patterns," which limited patient options and created a consumer backlash in the 1990s.

In addition, unlike HMOs, the ACOs must meet a long list of quality measures to ensure they are not saving money by stinting on necessary care.

What Could Go Wrong?

Many health care economists fear that the race to form ACOs could have a significant downside: hospital mergers and provider consolidation. As hospitals position themselves to become integrated systems, many are joining forces and purchasing physician practices, leaving fewer independent hospitals and doctors. Greater market share gives these health systems more leverage in negotiations with insurers, which can drive up health costs and limit patient choice.

But Lieberman says while ACOs could accelerate the merger trend, consolidations are already "such a powerful and pervasive trend that it's a little like worrying about the calories I get when I eat the maraschino cherry on top of my hot fudge sundae. It's a serious public policy issue with or without ACOs."

Are ACOs the Future of Health Care?

ACOs are already becoming pervasive, but they may be just an interim step on the way to a more efficient American health care system. "ACOs aren't the end game," says Chas Roades, chief research officer at The Advisory Board Company in Washington.

One of the key challenges for hospitals and physicians is that the incentives in ACOs are to reduce hospital stays, emergency room visits and expensive specialist and testing services—all the ways that hospitals and physicians make money in the fee-for-service system, explains Roades.

He says the ultimate goal would be for providers to take on full financial responsibility for caring for a population of patients for a fixed payment, but that will require a transition beyond ACOs.

Doctors and Patients Take Matters into Their Own Hands

Algorithms for Innovation

Algorithms for Innovation was designed to spark conversations, highlight best practices, and foster collaboration to help transform the future.

The path to a good outcome is hardly straightforward. Anywhere along the way, systems and behaviors can advance patients forward or set them back. Government metrics tried to ensure safe passage, but 1,700 checklist boxes later, no one is satisfied. Patients and providers are starting to take matters into their own hands and hold each other accountable.

You won't hear William Couldwell, M.D., Ph.D., utter the phrase "It's not brain surgery," because most of the time it is. Chair of the Department of Neurosurgery, Couldwell travels the world training other neurosurgeons and spending as many as 12 hours in the operating room working against the odds of a ruptured aneurysm or teasing out tumors that tangle dangerously close to critical brain tissue.

When one of his patients wakes up from surgery and takes perhaps the most grateful breath of her life, she next wants to know "Can I still see?" "Can I hear?" "Do I recognize the person sitting at the side of my bed?" But those are not the metrics that will measure Couldwell's performance. Instead, 15 years of education and training and 30 years of experience will be measured by a cascade of hospital, government and insurance company metrics—from the routine (quick administration of antibiotics and catheter removal) to the practical (the speed with which the patient is upon her feet and sent home or to a skilled nursing facility). Doctors, residents and nurses will check off hundreds of boxes pre- and post-surgery that will be used for rankings, accreditation, reimbursement and, in some cases, nothing at all.

What they won't measure, at least not yet, is what's really important: the improvement in a patient's quality of life, his ability to go back to work or her joy at being alive to see a child married or a grandchild born. "We take away the threat to a patient's life or extend someone's life," says Couldwell, "but none of these metrics asks questions that would capture that."

At the same time, metrics have improved medical outcomes, cut costs and saved lives. We've needed some way to justify, quantify, measure and control what we're doing, especially in light of the Institute of Medicine's estimate that roughly 30 percent of US health care spending is squandered on unnecessary, poorly delivered or wasteful care. For the most part, the federal government has taken on that responsibility, creating more than 1,700 quality and safety metrics.

The problem is that metrics are designed to simplify, but health is incredibly complex. How a person feels, ultimately, cannot be measured by adherence to processes. It's deeply personal and variable. The other problem is that, like so many patriarchal traditions in medicine, providers, systems, government and payers have all taken a we-know-best approach and left out one important voice—presumably, the very person to whom the outcome matters most—the patient.

But that's changing.

Inviting the Patient In

Three years ago, Marge Torina was working in her yard, scraping a pile of leaves out from under the porch. It might have been the flip-flops. It could have been the tools, or both. But she tripped. And whatever the cause of her fall, Torina couldn't get up. She scooted across the dirt, yelling to catch the attention of a dog walker nearby who called an ambulance. She had shattered her hip and ended up with a 17-inch rod in her leg.

When she transferred to University of Utah Health's Rehabilitation Center, rather than starting with a standardized program, her therapist asked about her life and her goals for recovery. The team then created a regimen tailored for an Italian matriarch who wanted, more than anything, to be able to cook Sunday dinner for her family. Instead of putting her on the stationary bike, the therapists took her grocery shopping with a group of patients and then put her somewhere she loved—the kitchen. She spent the next couple of hours making her signature summer pasta, a celebration of hot-weather bounty—vine-ripened tomatoes, black olives, onion, basil and "lots of cheese"—and proudly served it up to hungry staff. The next therapy session, she made pizzelles, delicate anise-flavored holiday cookies. Three years and countless Sunday dinners later, 80-year-old Torina remembers her rehabilitation with fondness. "It was fun," she says. "It was better than going down there and doing exercises. And it was a lot of training for when I did eventually get home."

"Patients find motivation and hope when thinking about being able to do the things that bring joy to their lives," says Occupational Therapist Christopher Noren. "So that's what we focus on. Rather than routine exercise and set programs, we try to tap into intrinsic motivation and the things that matter most to each individual."

For professional superbike racer Shane Turpin, that was getting back on his bike. The 49-year-old had taken the weekend off to ride dirt bikes with friends when he shorted a jump and landed awkwardly. He managed to save the landing but he could feel bones moving in his boots. He'd broken the tibia and fibula in both legs. His ankles were shattered.

The first doctors he saw gave him grim news: He would never walk or compete again. Three hospitals later, he ended up at U of U Health. With amputation the only other option, Turpin wanted surgery immediately. "I didn't care about the consequences, I just needed my legs."

After five operations—and two months of intense, home-based rehab involving a training bike on rollers—Turpin hit the track and set the fastest lap of the day. "I'm not 100 percent. But I'm close. I'm going faster than I ever have, and I'm almost 50."

Finding the Sweet Spot

"Every day we're trying to figure out what a patient wants to do, what the provider can do for them, and if there's a match," says Charles Saltzman, M.D., chair of the Department of Orthopaedic Surgery. Consider the options for a 60-year-old patient with end-stage arthritis: the surgeon could fuse the ankle and the patient's pain would abate, but he would have a hard time walking up and down hills. Replacing the ankle would provide better function but limit high-impact exercise. "Finding out what the patient's goals and expectations are is a critical part of being a good doctor," says Saltzman.

As a health care system, Saltzman admits, we haven't been very good at asking patients what they want or sorting out how well they function before or after treatment. So in 2009, he started doing just that. The Department of Orthopaedics launched an early version of the NIH's Patient-Reported Outcomes Measurement Information System (PROMIS) and then worked with a U of U Health team to create a customized, patient-friendly tool called mEVAL Personal Health Assessment. Patients can fill out an online assessment before their appointments or complete a brief computer adaptive questionnaire on an iPad when they get to the clinic. Questions range from their level of pain and social support to whether they have feelings of depression and anxiety. These patient-reported outcomes (PROs) provide physicians with critical information that can be used at the point of care, says Saltzman, especially when dealing with a patient who isn't a good communicator. They also help track progress over time and help the clinician and patient understand if that progress is appropriate based on data collected on other patients with similar problems.

Today in 30 clinic waiting rooms at U of U Health, patients are tapping on iPads before their appointments, reporting on their functional, psychological and pain status. The number of patients completing the questionnaires has doubled to nearly 13,000 per month. And by the end of 2018, PROs, including pre-visit emails and mid- and post-treatment questionnaires, will be used throughout the system. Not only will the information guide patient-physician discussions and help providers individualize treatment, it will also provide a resource for researchers to look more broadly at outcomes.

"We finally have a systematic way to listen to our patients," says Senior Vice President for Health Sciences Vivian S. Lee, M.D., Ph.D., M.B.A. "That gives us the opportunity to marry that information with our expertise to personalize their care and, ultimately, to begin measuring outcomes in terms of what is important to patients."

Shifting Responsibility, Just a Little

Thomas Varghese, M.D., M.S., associate professor of thoracic surgery, makes his expectations clear from the first consultation with a lung cancer patient: Stop smoking or find another surgeon. With his Surgery Strive program, modeled after the Strong for Surgery program he helped found at the University of Washington, Varghese has his patients sign a contract of sorts, agreeing to make the lifestyle changes necessary to improve their surgery outcomes. He'll refer you to the wellness clinic to get your blood sugar in check. And he'll help you quit smoking—provide you with nicotine patches, write a prescription for Chantix or sign you up for a cessation program. But he will not operate on you if you're smoking. A simple blood test will show if you're lying.

It's not as paternalistic or heartless as it sounds. For years, doctors cajoled and urged their patients to exercise and quit smoking. But changing patient behavior is more a lifelong campaign than a pre-surgery project. "Patients are adults," says Varghese. "It's about having hard conversations and sharing in the decision-making."

Varghese knows some of his patients may sign under duress and others will look for another surgeon. But eventually, he figures, all surgeons will be holding patients accountable in the same way. He may be right. This year, the American College of Surgeons adopted the pre-surgery checklists as standard procedure. Britain's National

Health Service took it a step further. In September, it announced it would block obese patients with BMIs over 30 and smokers from most surgeries—including routine hip and knee operations.

Partnerships and Mind Shifts

Of course, measuring a successful outcome for a hip replacement, a round of chemotherapy or a baby's birth is much easier than defining a good medical result for chronic conditions. "For years, we've been stuck in a plumber model of health care," says Sam Finlayson, M.D., M.P.H., chair of surgery. "Fixing the faucet when it blows generates a lot of revenue but doesn't necessarily make patients better long term. Reversing a long, slow, recurring 'leak'— like diabetes or heart failure—or preventing it in the first place, is a much more difficult thing to incentivize." Care for patients with chronic conditions—many of them elderly—can be particularly fragmented with multiple specialists and no one held responsible for the overall health of the patient.

"As we begin to move away from the old fee-for-service model, providers will become heavily accountable for patients' overall health, not just the outcome of a specific surgery or illness," says Mark Supiano, M.D., director of the University of Utah's Center on Aging. "Taking on that responsibility will require a reset in the way that many physicians and systems think." It also will force systems to form new partnerships across the continuum of care. Working with an interdisciplinary team, Supiano's created a new "medical home" designed to break down the physical and technological barriers that plague communication between hospitalists, post-acute care centers and primary care physicians.

A New Way of Thinking

With new payment models and shifting responsibility for outcomes, we have to relearn how to talk to each other. Finlayson calls it the "dialectic" between providers and patients, a shared responsibility for the way we work together to maximize medical outcomes.

Others agree. "We tend to throw the onus on the other party, but we need to recognize that patients often don't have the resources—intellectually, emotionally or financially—to align their lives to what their medical care team is trying to educate them to do," says Nate Gladwell, R.N., M.H.A., director of telehealth for U of U Health. "We can prescribe, we can educate, we can diagnose all we want. But at the end of the day, health care is a partnership," he says. "It's going to take all of us."

[...]

US Health Care Is a Privilege, Not a Right

Agence France-Presse (AFP)

Agence France-Presse is an international news agency headquartered in Paris, France.

I n 1944, president Franklin Roosevelt urged Congress to pass a "second bill of rights." Number six on the list was "the right to adequate medical care and the opportunity to achieve and enjoy good health."

Seventy-three years later, despite the passage of many health care reforms, his dream remains as controversial as it was back then.

Under former president Barack Obama, more than 20 million previously uninsured Americans gained health care coverage. Those who would have once had to sell their homes to pay for cancer treatments or limited doctors' visits because of the cost gained at least some peace of mind.

But in the land of rugged individualism, health care has never attained the status of fundamental right, unlike education. Health insurance is simply a product like any other, say Republicans who, under the leadership of President Donald Trump, are trying to repeal most of Obamacare, the landmark law signed in 2010.

Private System

After World War II, the idea of national health insurance supported by Roosevelt's successor Harry Truman ran into the new geopolitical reality. Opponents called it "socialized medicine."

"It's the beginning of the Cold War, we're terrified of Stalin and Communism. The word socialism carried a lot of baggage," University of Michigan medical historian Howard Markel said. "Truman wrote in his memoirs that it was one of the most disappointing political defeats of his career."

"In the US, health care a privilege, not a right," by Agence France-Presse, Inquirer.net, May 6, 2017. Reprinted by permission.

Most Americans receive health insurance from their employers, under a system in which workers are covered by an arrangement largely negotiated directly between employers and trade unions.

"If you look at the systems in France, Germany and Britain, there was an architect of the system," said Melissa Thomasson, a professor of economics at Miami University in Ohio.

"In our country, we have a very piecemeal system" under the control of insurance companies, the pharmaceutical industry, employers and doctors, all determined to limit the government's role.

Persistent Faults

But the market doesn't cover everyone.

In 1965, president Lyndon Johnson wrangled a compromise with Congress to create Medicare, public health insurance for over people over 65, and Medicaid for the poor and disabled, initially mainly women with children.

Still, health care was seen as a privilege which recipients are worthy of deserving through poverty, age or contributions. Poor bachelors, for example, are excluded from Medicaid because they're considered able to work.

"A large number of Americans believe in individual responsibility," said Thomas William O'Rourke, professor emeritus in the Department of Kinesiology and Community Health at the University of Illinois.

"We have never said that health care is a right," he added. "We have said you will get health care if you fall into a certain group," such as military veterans or native Americans.

In the following decades, the battle lines of the ideological debate hardly shifted between the left, supporting universal coverage, and the right, which opposes the idea for budgetary reasons and as a matter of principle.

In 1993, president Bill Clinton and his wife Hillary launched an effort to reform the health care system, a tangle of public regulations and private providers, in order to cover everyone.

The attempt failed spectacularly.

When Congress passed Obama's bill in 2010, it succeeded by a hair. Not a single Republican supported it.

Obamacare instituted tax incentives, mandatory coverage requirements and financial assistance for millions. But it never called into question the system's private foundations.

Utopia

"It's part of the DNA of the United States to somehow maintain choice in health care insurance plans," said Howard Bauchner, editor in chief of the *Journal of the American Medical Association*.

However, "the irony of the free market system is that it doesn't work in health care very well."

The reality is that the industry is steadily consolidating and competition weakening. Incentives aren't enough: more than 25 million people still lack health insurance. At the same time, spending on health care continues mounting rapidly because the government has little control over fees charged.

To address those faults, left-wing figures such as Bernie Sanders advocate the kind of national public health care system that Europeans enjoy.

Or, as Hillary Clinton once pragmatically said, a utopia that will "never, ever come to pass."

CHAPTER 4

Will the Quality of Care Suffer with Universal Health Care?

Linking Health to Other Areas of Life

Sustainable Development Solutions Network (SDSN)

The Sustainable Development Solutions Network aims to accelerate joint learning and promote integrated approaches that address the interconnected economic, social, and environmental challenges confronting the world.

[…]

Linking Health to Other Development Goals

Health is both a pre-condition for and an outcome of sustainable development and relates to all four pillars of sustainable development (economic, social, environmental, and governance). It is universally recognized that several critical determinants of health and illness lie outside the health sector. Education, finance, agriculture, food processing, trade and investment, environment, urban design, transport, communications, law and human rights are some of the many areas where actions can enable or erode health. Health impacts several core dimensions of development. A sick child cannot go to school and malnourished students perform poorly in academics as well as sports. A sick employee either stays away from work ("absenteeism") or underperforms after turning up ("presenteeism"), affecting overall economic performance. At the level of household economics, poor health impoverishes families through costs for care, lost wages, and even permanent loss of employment. Long periods of illness lead to stress and domestic strife within households. For all of these reasons, every SDG should consider pro-health strategies. Achieving Health and Wellbeing at All Ages is impossible without intersectoral action and enabling policies that link diverse SDSN priorities. Some key areas of intersection are described below.

Thematic Network on Health for All. "Health in the Framework of Sustainable Development." New York: Sustainable Development Solutions Network (SDSN), 2014. Full text available online at www.unsdsn.org. Reprinted by permission.

Health and Its Relationship with the Eradication of Extreme Poverty and Hunger

Poverty, at multiple levels, continues to be the most formidable challenge to improvements in health. The World Food Program estimates that 870 million people go to bed hungry each day, and 45% of under-5 mortality is caused by poor nutrition. Micronutrient deficiency is further responsible for much morbidity in children and adults. The SDGs must therefore prioritize the eradication of hunger, a key component of improving global health. Repeated infections, such as diarrhea in childhood, leave behind a legacy of serious, lifelong health problems such as stunted growth and impaired cognitive development, with further implications on work opportunities and overall productivity. In HICs and LMICs, the increasing cost of healthcare and rising out-of-pocket spending (OOPS) burdens households; in many regions healthcare costs are a major reason for households falling below the poverty line. Poor nations are unable to afford publically financed healthcare services for their populations and often rely on donor support, especially to reach vulnerable populations. In the absence of adequate resources, LMICs have had to adopt "targeted" instead of universalistic approaches that often miss those in greatest need. By prioritizing UHC in the post-2015 development agenda, and with adequate resources, we can transform households impoverished by healthcare costs into resilient households that are active in the community. Over time, as poverty is reduced and incomes rise, countries will need to rely less and less on donor support and will eventually be able to finance UHC.

[…]

Health and Its Relationship with Ensuring Effective Learning for All Children and Youth

Education and health are profoundly linked; both are human rights and are inputs into human capital. Better education contributes to better health, through increased employment generating income, increasing the ability of households to afford better nutrition and healthcare. There is abundant evidence from across the world that education positively impacts the health status of individuals within countries, even independent of income. Education, especially women's education, is another key investment with a direct impact on family planning, child health and development, and family nutrition. This is because education increases awareness of risk factors, health seeking and health utilization behaviors. In turn, better health has significant impact on education. As discussed, healthy, well-nourished children do better in school. Stunting from under-nutrition in early childhood has been shown to have an impact on IQ and cognitive development, affecting learning and long-term career prospects. Vaccines have the power to transform lives, giving children a chance to grow up healthy, go to school, and improve their life prospects. The relationships between education and health are vital and cannot be ignored. In the post-2015 agenda, it is crucial that synergies between education and health be realized, such as described in the SDSN report "An Action Agenda for Sustainable Development."[1]

Universal education for all children must be advanced vigorously, and health literacy could be fast-tracked through mass media and settings-based non-formal health education. A variety of communication channels and social networks can be used for this purpose. Increasing the health literacy of young persons is an especially high priority to empower the global citizens of the 21st century with the knowledge, motivation and skills needed to help them to protect personal health and act as societal change agents for promoting population health. Youth-friendly health education is especially important in preventing unwanted pregnancy and the spread of HIV/AIDS, teaching values of human rights and gender equity, and encouraging healthy habits such as healthy diets, physical activity, and the prevention of alcohol, tobacco, and drug use throughout the life course.

Health and Its Relationship with Achieving Gender Equality, Social Inclusion, and Human Rights for All

UHC will be a significant step in realizing the right to health for all. UHC ensures equality in coverage and access to health services for all people. However, social policy at the national level cannot be successful without recognizing within-household and within-country inequalities based on discrimination due to gender, race, ethnicity, age, disability, religion, sexual orientation, refugee status, or other status. It is therefore important that health indicators are disaggregated and achievements between groups be compared to ensure equity in improvements. Where there are gaps in achievement between groups, countries must implement policies to ensure the closing of such gaps. In some instances this will require innovative programs to address cultural barriers to consuming health services. Further, by ensuring equity in both access to and utilization of health services by all people, inequalities in other sectors such as employment will be reduced. In addition, the post-2015 development agenda should call on countries to address assault and violence against women and other marginalized groups (including sexual violence), violent crime, female genital mutilation, service provision for displaced and refugee communities, and other determinants of health that are driven by political and/or cultural factors. Sexual and reproductive health and rights are especially critical, as women and girls bear the brunt of sexual and reproductive health problems. The primary health care system, as part of the delivery of SRH services, should ensure detection and comprehensive responses to gender-based violence, offering a package of critical services to victims/survivors.[2]

Gender, Health Systems and Knowledge Translation

Early marriage and related teenage pregnancies are a result of highly unequal gender relations and discrimination against girls and women. WHO reports that complications from pregnancy and childbirth are the leading cause of death among girls aged 15-

19 years in many low- and middle-income countries. Stillbirths and newborn deaths are 50% higher among infants born to adolescent mothers than among those born to mothers aged 20-29 years. Health policies and programs that focus merely on institutional deliveries ignore these facts. In 2008, a project in Koppal, Karnataka (India), combined a nuanced gendered framework to strengthen evidence and advocacy to reduce maternal morbidity, mortality and violence against women. The project's verbal autopsies of maternal deaths and near misses since 2008 revealed systemic failures and the need for accountability in obstetric care and health systems that fuelled high levels of maternal mortality despite rising rates of institutional delivery.

[...]

Health and Its Relationship with Empowering Inclusive, Productive and Resilient Cities

The growth of cities and progressive urbanization of the global population presents challenges as well as opportunities for health. The urban poor suffer daily deprivations of shelter and food security, with millions living in slums and squatter settlements prone to water and sanitation-related diseases. Urban dwellers, rich and poor, are at greater risk of harmful health behaviors like smoking, alcohol and drug use, diseases like TB and dengue fever, and road traffic injuries, relative to their rural counterparts. Urban populations, particularly those residing in unplanned housing or densely populated areas, are disproportionately affected by environmental disasters.

Services related to the provision of clean water supply (for drinking and hygiene), sanitation, green spaces, community recreational facilities, protected cycling lanes, safe pedestrian paths, traffic safety, pollution control and public protection from crime are among the health needs that the SDSN's Thematic Group on Sustainable Cities address in their report. It is important that UHC also be realized in urban settings, as a complement to better city planning policies. The health needs of rural to urban migrants and slum communities need particular attention, particularly as spatial design is developed for accessible primary health care through suitably located community health centers. The SDGs are an opportunity for health-friendly urbanization and to invest in gathering greater evidence on the costs and benefits of urbanization on human health.[3]

[…]

Notes

1. More information on the linkages between health and education can be found in the Report of the SDSN Thematic Group on Early Childhood Development, Education and Learning, and Transition to Work entitled *The Future Of Our Children: Lifelong, Multi-Generational Learning For Sustainable Development.* www.unsdsn.org/resources.

2. More information on the linkages between health and social inclusion can be found in the Report of the SDSN Thematic Group on Challenges of Social Inclusion: Gender, Inequalities, and Human Rights entitled *Achieving Gender Equality, Social Inclusion, and Human Rights for All: Challenges and Priorities for the Sustainable Development Agenda.* www.unsdsn.org/resources.

3. For more information, see the publications from the SDSN Thematic Group on Sustainable Cities: Inclusive, Resilient, and Connected at http://unsdsn.org/thematicgroups/tg9.

Select Services with Universal Health Care

Peter C. Smith and Kalipso Chalkidou

Peter C. Smith is an emeritus professor of health policy at Imperial College London. Kalipso Chalkidou is the Director of Global Health Policy and a senior fellow at the Center for Global Development.

The World Health Organization identifies three dimensions of policymaking choices as countries seek to implement universal health coverage (UHC): the groups in the population to be covered, the level of financial protection offered when seeking access to services, and the range of services to be covered. Of these, the first two dimensions frequently offer little realistic scope for policy variation. Allowing access only to certain population subgroups contradicts the fundamental intent of universality. And imposing any level of user charges may exclude access for the poorest groups, as well as entail administrative complexity. Therefore, the central focus of policy will usually be the third dimension of the UHC design: the range of services to be made available, usually referred to as the health benefits package (HBP).

Many high-income countries have sought to maintain packages that are quite comprehensive, in the sense that most clinically accepted interventions have been included.[1] In contrast, low- and middle-income countries with slender resources have been forced to confront the issue of which interventions or services to include in their benefits package.[2] Sometimes, as, for example, in the case of Chile[3] or Mexico,[4] this problem has been addressed directly, and a carefully circumscribed package has been explicitly defined. More often, however, the package has been developed piecemeal and implicitly, as, for example, in India.[5]

"Should Countries Set an Explicit Health Benefits Package? The Case of the English National Health Service," by Peter C. Smith and Kalipso Chalkidou, International Society for Pharmacoeconomics and Outcomes Research, 2016. https://www.ispor.org/universal-health-care-coverage_benefits-package_ENH.pdf. Licensed under CC BY 4.0.

Numerous techniques and processes have been adopted for selecting the benefits package.[6] Nevertheless, whatever the resources available, policymakers will usually wish to maximize the effectiveness of their UHC policy, in the form of maximizing the "value" (however defined) of the health services purchased with the limited publicly funded budget. Economists have advocated the use of cost-effectiveness analysis (CEA) as making this principle operational, on the assumption that the objective to be maximized is health gain. Although the application of the cost-effectiveness criterion suffers from some theoretical limitations, it has enjoyed widespread acceptance as a reasonable principle for prioritizing the use of scarce health service resources.[7]

[...]

Arguments For and Against Setting an Explicit HBP

As documented by Glassman et al.,[8] there are numerous well-rehearsed arguments in favor of setting an explicit HBP to which all beneficiaries are entitled:

1. It creates explicit entitlements for patients, whose access to services might otherwise be largely determined by clinical professionals, with the consequent potential for arbitrary variations in access.

2. It helps to identify whether *funds are being spent wisely* on services that create the maximum benefit for the society.

3. By specifying the services to be delivered, it facilitates important *resource allocation decisions*, such as regional funding allocations, and other planning functions, creating a precondition for reducing variations in care and outcomes.

4. It facilitates orderly *adherence to budget limits*, which might otherwise be attained only through arbitrary restrictions on access and services.

5. It reduces the risk that providers will require *informal payments* from patients to secure access to high-value services.

6. The entitlements created empower *poor and marginalized groups*, who cannot be made aware of any specific entitlement without an explicit HBP.

7. It creates the preconditions for a market in *complementary health insurance* for services not covered, with a number of potential benefits for the health system as a whole.

It is important to distinguish between explicitness in stating the contents of the benefits package and consistency and rigor in selecting the contents. It is quite conceivable that a package may be made explicit, but the process for selecting the contents is opaque and inconsistent. Some of the aforementioned virtues of an explicit package arise whatever may be the selection process. Nevertheless, most can have full effect only if the package is selected using consistent application of an explicit set of criteria.

Notwithstanding the powerful reasons for developing an explicit benefits package, and basing it on consistent stated criteria, there are also reasons for caution in pursuing an explicitly delineated package:

1. There are very significant practical *difficulties of specifying a package* in enough detail to have an impact on clinicians. Although it may be feasible to make broad statements regarding the services to be delivered, it may be impractical to specify the circumstances in which specific treatments may be funded. This may be because of a lack of suitable evidence and analytic capacity, a lack of adequate information systems or funding mechanisms, or a lack of detailed clinical guidelines on what constitutes best care.

2. A closely defined package may *inhibit innovation*, especially if it is based on treatments to be delivered rather than on disease categories. If the package is not constantly reviewed and updated, there is a risk that it

will reflect outdated approaches to care, and ignore new, more efficient treatments or modes of delivering care, and inhibit take-up of those new approaches.

3. In the same vein, the package may *inhibit warranted variations in treatment* that reflect patients' circumstances or preferences. The contents of any package will be based on broad average responses to treatment in the population at risk. Although it is important that all treatments should be cost-effective, there will often be circumstances in which clinical judgment may suggest departures from usual treatment for specific patients that improve cost-effectiveness. In principle, any package should be flexible enough to accommodate such departures.

4. Explicit statements of patient entitlement may *create serious political and legal difficulties* for health ministries, by appearing to favor certain groups at the expense of others and giving rise to a sense that some health care is being "rationed." Of course, the prime reason for the limitations to care is created by the limited budget made available, but that may not be the focus of political debate. In such circumstances, however, a ministry may be prepared to sacrifice improved efficiency by retaining some ambiguity about the nature of the package.

5. There may be *existing rigidities in health system* that preclude moving toward a new package of care. The transition may require investment costs in new infrastructure and training, may cause disruption to the care of existing patients, may entail disinvestment from some services, and may require political and clinical leadership. Furthermore, there may be an asymmetry between the willingness to pay for new programs compared with established programs.[9] Such concerns are particularly important when the innovation has a substantial budgetary impact.[10] They are common to most health system reforms and require careful planning

to ensure a smooth transition over time toward the new arrangements.

6. A benefits package may create an *uncertain financial liability* for the health system. By creating entitlements to care, it becomes impossible to limit access through waiting times, user fees, or other informal means. Although this is of course the intention behind creating the package, it may mean that the impact on the UHC budget is uncertain, and if not underpinned by good analysis, the sustainability of the UHC program may be compromised.

[...]

Conclusions

In the "Introduction" we listed seven benefits of setting an explicit HBP. Several policy problems in the NHS can therefore be attributed, at least in part, to the absence of an explicit HBP. Some of the specific problems are as follows:

1. *Explicit entitlements.* There are few firm entitlements to treatment for patients, and access to many services relies on the variable policies of local commissioners and practitioners.

2. *Spending funds wisely.* It is very difficult to determine whether commissioners are spending their funds in a way that maximizes health benefits for society.

3. *Resource allocation decisions.* NICE is making an increasingly important contribution to the improvement of allocative efficiency in the NHS at the level of individual treatments. Nevertheless, geographical resource allocation decisions are hampered by a lack of an explicit statement of the services to be provided.

4. *Adherence to budget limits.* Budget discipline is strong by international standards. It is, however, achieved

by various somewhat arbitrary means, and the lack of an HBP has led to a "postcode" lottery of access to some services.

5. *Informal payments.* With a few exceptions, providers do not require either formal or informal payments from patients in the NHS. Nevertheless, local limitations to access for some services may encourage patients to seek private care, where they can afford it, which must be funded from voluntary private insurance or out-of-pocket.

6. *Poor and marginalized groups.* There is considerable evidence that poor access to services is greatest among disadvantaged social groups, a problem that an explicit HBP may help to address.[11]

7. *Complementary health insurance.* There is no significant market in complementary health insurance for services not covered by the NHS. Instead, there is a small but significant market for duplicate private insurance, which seeks to bypass services provided by the NHS through lower waiting times and enhanced convenience. This market has the potential to undermine support for the NHS if it attracts larger numbers of richer people.

Nevertheless, rather than suggesting an absence of an HBP, the English example more accurately highlights variations in the "hardness" of the HBP specification. At one extreme, NICE technology appraisals rule in (or rule out) specific technologies in their entirety (albeit sometimes possibly limited to certain patient subgroups) without reference to local provider circumstances. At the other extreme, a mass of clinical guidelines offers clinical recommendations based on existing evidence but offer no direct incentives to comply. At an intermediate level, there are clinical practices that are embodied in performance measures that suggest good practice and that may indirectly therefore affect provider reputation and revenue. They, however, do not directly contain statements of patient entitlements, and NHS decision makers may need to balance the need to comply with performance metrics against the budgetary limits that have been set.

These variations in explicitness of the HBP may, to a large extent, reflect limitations in the evidence on the effectiveness and appropriateness of certain treatments. Such limitations suggest that there may be a need to adopt a nuanced approach to setting an explicit HBP. At one extreme, when the quality of information about the costs and benefits of a treatment is good, and there is little heterogeneity in patient needs and preferences, it may be possible to make very clear statements about entitlements. For many treatments, where there is less reliable information, it may be necessary to allow "exceptions" from usual practice, which require an explicit statement or request from the clinician. Furthermore, theory suggests that treatments for which evidence is weak should be subject to a more demanding cost-effectiveness threshold.[12] Of course, whatever degree of hardness is adopted in an HBP specification, it will always be important to have an accurate assessment of its likely budgetary impact.

It is noteworthy that many recent initiatives in England are seeking to impose greater uniformity through guidelines, performance measures, and payment mechanisms. At the same time, there have been some moves toward increased local autonomy, for example, in the devolution of responsibilities and funding to certain cities such as Manchester. These apparently conflicting developments reflect the continuing tension between uniformity and local flexibility found in most health systems. Yet it is important to note that there are efforts to define health packages, often in the form of "essential" levels of services, even in decentralized health systems such as those found in Italy, Finland, and Sweden. There is a need for a clearly specified national HBP so that local decision makers can be held properly to account for their choices.

Thus, the fact that there is no formal HBP in England should not be interpreted as a suggestion that seeking to create such a package is infeasible or undesirable. Many of the policy problems confronted by NHS policymakers would to some extent be eased by the creation of a more explicit HBP. There are, however, many practical and political constraints to pursuing greater clarity, and there will always be a need to retain some flexibility in the services made available. Perhaps the biggest challenge to creating an explicit HBP is the concern that it would create unaffordable entitlements to care and conflict with the local flexibility needed to adhere to budgets. This concern, however, may arise more from the unaffordable contents of the package rather than from the principle of setting out entitlements clearly.

As health systems seek to make a transition toward UHC, they must confront the issue of whether and how to establish an explicit benefits package, which sets out the treatments and services to which beneficiaries can secure access. Arrangements must also be put in place to ensure adequate quality of the services contained in the package. English policymakers have traditionally shied away from explicit specification of an HBP for various reasons. There are, nevertheless, signs that they may be moving toward an "intelligent" HBP, specified through instruments such as the NICE essential medicines list, broader treatment guidelines, performance measures, and payment mechanisms. The key challenge is to maintain an appropriate balance between clarity (when the evidence warrants) and flexibility (when it does not). Although there are important reasons why setting out an explicit HBP may be technically, administratively, and politically difficult, we suggest that, on the basis of the English experience, the difficulties that arise from failing to set out the HBP far outweigh any advantages and that health systems should consider moving toward an explicitly specified HBP as an essential element of their UHC plans.

Notes

[1] Schreyögg J, Stargardt T, Velasco-Garrido M, Busse R. Defining the "health benefit basket" in nine European countries: evidence from the European Union Health BASKET Project. Eur J Health Econ 2015;6(Suppl. 1):2–10.

[2] Cotlear D, Nagpal S, Smith O, et al. Going Universal: How 24 Developing Countries Are Implementing Universal Health Coverage from the Bottom Up. Washington, DC: World Bank Publications, 2015.

[3] Missoni E, Solimano G. Towards Universal Health Coverage: The Chilean Experience. World Health Report (2010) Background Paper, No. 4. Geneva, Switzerland: World Health Organization, 2010.

[4] Bonilla-Chacín M, Aguilera N. The Mexican Social Protection System in Health. UNICO Studies Series 1. Washington, DC: World Bank, 2013.

[5] Forgia GL, Nagpal S. Government-Sponsored Health Insurance in India: Are You Covered? Directions in Development: Human Development. Washington, DC: World Bank, 2012.

[6] Glassman A, Chalkidou K. Priority-Setting in Health: Building Institutions for Smarter Public Spending. Washington, DC: Center for Global Development, 2013.

[7] Meltzer DO, Smith PC. Theoretical issues relevant to the economic evaluation of health technologies 1. In: Pauly M, Mcguire P, Barros PP, eds. Handbook of Health Economics. New York, NY: Elsevier, 2011. p. 433–69.

[8] Glassman A, Giedion U, Sakuma Y, Smith P. Defining a health benefits package: what are the necessary processes? Health Syst Reform 2016;2:1–12.

[9] O'Brien BJ, Gertsen K, Willan AR, Faulkner A. Is there a kink in consumers' threshold value for cost-effectiveness in health care? Health Econ 2002;11:175–80.

[10] Glassman A, Giedion U, Sakuma Y, Smith P. Defining a health benefits package: what are the necessary processes? Health Syst Reform 2016;2:1–12.

[11] Strategic Review of Health Inequalities in England. Fair Society, Healthy Lives. London: University College London, 2010.

[12] Palmer S, Smith P. Incorporating option values into the economic evaluation of health care technologies. J Health Econ 2000;19: 755–766.

Canada's Cautionary Tale of Universal Health Care

Candice Malcolm

Candice Malcolm is a syndicated columnist for the Toronto Sun *and the author of several books.*

I n the Netflix series *House of Cards*, President Frank Underwood campaigned for the White House by telling Americans, "You are entitled to nothing." The fictional president—a Democrat, no less—was forthright with American voters about the unaffordable and unsustainable structure of America's entitlement programs, and he was rewarded at the polls.

In real-life America, unfortunately, there is no such courageous honesty from the political class. Even many in the Republican party, once the stalwart force fighting against the growth of big government, are now resigned to contemplating a government takeover of the health-care industry in the wake of their failure to repeal and replace Obamacare. Charles Krauthammer, for example, woefully predicts that President Trump will opt for single-payer health care. F. H. Buckley, meanwhile, optimistically calls for Trump to look to the Canadian model of universal coverage.

There's just one problem: The Canadian model of universal coverage is failing.

Assessing Canada's Single-Payer System

The Canada Health Act (CHA), introduced in 1984, governs the complicated fiscal agreement between the provinces, who administer health services, and the feds, who manage their health-insurance monopoly and transfer funds to the local governments. Unlike in the United Kingdom, where health care is socialized and hospitals are run by the National Health Service, in Canada health care is technically delivered privately, although given the Kafkaesque regulations and restrictions that govern it, the system is by no means market-based. In fact, Canada's government-controlled health-care system has become more restrictive than communist China's.

Debates about health-care policy typically revolve around three key metrics: universality, affordability, and quality.

Canada passes the first test with flying colors: Every resident of the country is insured under the CHA, with covered procedures free at the point of delivery. While medical providers are independent from the federal government, they are compelled to accept CHA insurance—and nothing else—by a prohibition on accepting payments outside the national-insurance scheme so long as they wish to continue accepting federal health-transfer funds. The spigot of money from Ottawa thus ensures a de facto government monopoly in the health-insurance market.

The CHA provides and ensures universal coverage from the top down. In Canada, the government determines what procedures are medically necessary. Bureaucrats, not doctors, decide which procedures and treatments are covered under the CHA—based on data and statistics rather than on the needs of patients. While private insurance does exist—an OECD report found that 75 percent of Canadians have supplementary insurance—it applies only to procedures and services that fall outside the CHA—including dental work, optometric care, and pharmaceutical drugs.

When it comes to affordability, the Canadian system also passes, if just barely. Canadians pay for health insurance through their taxes; most never see a medical bill. But that doesn't mean the system is affordable. Au contraire, it relies almost entirely on current taxpayers to subsidize the disproportionately large health-care needs of elderly Canadians in their final few years of life. Rather than pre-funding the system to deal with the coming tsunami of aging Baby Boomers, Canada's provincial governments pay and borrow as they go—and rank among the most indebted sub-sovereign borrowers in the world. According to Don Drummond, an economist appointed by Ontario's Liberal government to help fix its finances, Canada's largest province is projected to see health-care costs soar to the point where they will consume 80 percent of the entire provincial budget by 2030, up from 46 percent in 2010.

In the meantime, to address scarcity in the health-care system, government central planners ration care and cap the number of procedures offered in a given year, leading to queues, longer wait times, and a deterioration in the quality of care. Speaking of which …

… When it comes to the final metric, quality of care, Canada lags behind most other developed Western nations. A 2014 report by the Commonwealth Fund ranked Canada tenth out of eleven wealthy countries (ahead of only the United States) in health-care quality and dead last in timeliness of care. The report showed that 29 percent of adult Canadians who fell ill and needed to see a specialist waited two months or longer, and 18 percent waited four months or longer, compared with 6 percent and 7 percent of Americans, respectively.

Canada's quality of care is poor, and it continues to deteriorate in the face of a looming fiscal crunch and further rationing. In Canada's single-payer system, citizens cannot pay directly for procedures, and they cannot purchase private insurance to cover services provided by the CHA. They must instead wait in line or seek health-care services outside the country.

The System's Mysteriously Enduring Popularity

Canadian health-care outcomes are relatively poor, and yet the state-controlled system is beloved by Canadians. A 2012 poll by Leger Marketing in Montreal found that 94 percent of Canadians consider universal health care "an important source of collective pride." The reasons for this are complicated.

First, there is a well-propagated, pernicious myth that Canadians are pioneers in health care and that access to care is a basic human right. The universality of the system has become a key part of Canada's national identity, thanks in no small part to propagandists who ignore the widespread suffering wrought by the CHA in order to paint the country as some sort of socialist utopia.

Second, the system's costs are hidden. Many Canadians—and many progressives abroad—like to think that health care is "free" in Canada, when in fact, Canadian taxpayers pay, on average, $10,500 per year for all their health-care needs. Canadians simply have no concept of how much the services they consume cost, since the CHA prohibits providers from ever showing patients a bill.

Finally, there is the fact that Canada's single-payer system is made possible only by an accident of geography: It is propped up by the US health-care industry next door, which provides a parallel private system for very sick and very rich Canadians while acting as the driving force for global medical innovation. Ultimately, the antidote for Canada's poor health outcomes and long wait times has been for Canadians to seek care elsewhere. Don't take my word for it. A few years ago, Dr. Martin Samuels, the founder of the neurology department at Harvard's Brigham and Women's Hospital, wrote in *Forbes* about his experiences as a visiting professor in Canada:

> The reason the Canadian health-care system works as well as it does (and that is not by any means optimal) is because 90 percent of the population is within driving distance of the United States where the privately insured can be Seattled, Minneapolised, Mayoed, Detroited, Chicagoed, Clevelanded, and Buffaloed, thus relieving the pressure by the rich and influential to change a system that works well enough for the other people but not for them, especially when they are worried or in pain.
>
> In the United States, there is no analogous safety valve, so the influential simply demand a different level of care and receive it.

In other words, Canada's rigid state monopoly on health insurance works only because Canadians secretly have a private alternative: America's market-based system. It isn't just "rich and influential" Canadians who seek treatment in the US, either. In a recent government document obtained by the *Toronto*

Star, five stem-cell-transplant directors laid out the "crisis" in Ontario, revealing that "the health ministry approved more than $100 million in spending recently to redirect hundreds of patients who will probably die waiting for transplants in Ontario to hospitals in Cleveland, Buffalo, and Detroit." Likewise, a recent report from the Fraser Institute, Canada's leading public-policy think tank, estimated that more than 52,000 Canadians received medical treatment outside of Canada in 2014.

Canadians might like their single-payer health-care system in theory, but in practice, large numbers of them are going elsewhere for care.

Universal Suffering

As previously mentioned, the three key indicators to consider in evaluating a health-care system are universality, affordability, and quality. It's often said that you can have two out of the three, but you cannot have all three. The Canadian model offers universality, affordability, and the illusion of quality. But an illusion is all it is: The more closely you look, the worse the quality of Canadian health care appears.

As policymakers in Washington continue to debate the future of American health care, they might want to consider another quote from the cynical President Underwood before giving in to temptation, following Canada's lead, and pursuing a single-payer system: "Pay attention to the fine print. It's far more important than the selling price."

Universal Health Coverage
Contributes to Better Health

Organisation for Economic Co-operation and Development (OECD)

The Organisation for Economic Co-operation and Development provides a forum in which governments can work together to share experiences and seek solutions to common problems. They work with governments to understand what drives economic, social, and environmental change.

[...]

Universal Health Coverage Improves Health

Life Expectancy Has a Positive Correlation with Core Components of Health Coverage, as well as Overall Healthcare Resources

That UHC improves health outcomes makes intuitive sense—it helps ensure everyone in a society can use health services when they need them. But looking at the data gives a more precise idea of the impact of UHC on health.

For a selection of OECD countries and emerging economies (Brazil, China, Colombia, Costa Rica, India, Indonesia and Russia), a clear positive association exists between life expectancy at birth and UHC indicators reflecting the three core components of health coverage—the population covered by a core set of services (population coverage); out-of-pocket payments (financial coverage); GP density (service coverage)— as well as total health expenditures (as an overall health coverage proxy).

In particular:

- A positive correlation exists between population coverage and life expectancy, though this is mostly driven by India and Indonesia.

"Universal Health Coverage And Health Outcomes," Organisation for Economic Co-operation and Development, July 22, 2016. Reprinted by permission.

- A clear negative relationship exists between out-of-pocket (OOP) payments and life expectancy, suggesting that financial risk protection is associated with health outcomes.
- GP density (service coverage) is positively associated with life expectancy.
- The relationship between total health expenditure and life expectancy is also positive, though the United States stands out as an outlier.

Greater Spending on Health Has Made a Major Contribution to Better Health Outcomes, but the Wider Determinants of Health Are Also Important

Increased spending on health (a proxy for overall health coverage) has provided a significant contribution to life expectancy gains in recent decades. However, the wider determinants of health are also important, as new OECD analysis shows (James et al, forthcoming). Analysis of data across OECD countries for the period 1990 to 2013 shows that:

- Increased health spending contributed to about 1 year of observed life expectancy gains;
- Education was also a key driver, with expanded coverage contributing a further 1.19 years;
- Higher incomes contributed 0.81 years;
- Reductions in air pollution contributed to about a 1 year gain in life expectancy, with access to improved sanitation facilities a further 0.12 years;
- Behavioural aspects are also important. In particular, reduced smoking contributed a further gain of 0.55 years, with reduced alcohol consumption adding 0.08 years (note: increased obesity rates had a counterintuitive positive correlation with life expectancy, but this depended on the exact level of national income).

These results also hold true in low- and middle-income countries, although the magnitude of effects of these factors differs.

In particular, income and education were found to have a much larger effect in low- to middle-income countries.

A fundamental policy message emerging from this analysis is that coordinated action is required across ministries responsible for education, income, social protection and the environment, alongside health ministries. Partnerships with the private sector will also be important, particularly in relation to working conditions. Such collaborations can maximise the health impact of expanded health coverage.

Countries' Experiences Demonstrate the Positive Impact of Universal Health Coverage on Health Outcomes

A number of earlier studies have produced consistent findings to the new data analysis presented in this report. For example:

- Across 153 countries for the period 1995-2008, a 10% increase in government spending on health was associated with an average reduction in under-five mortality by 7.9 deaths per 1000 and adult mortality by 1.6 (women) and 1.3 (men) deaths per 1000 (Moreno-Serra & Smith, 2012).
- A 10% increase in government health expenditure per head led to reductions of 2.5-4.2% in mortality for children younger than 5 years and 4.2-5.2% reductions in maternal mortality rates (Bokhari, Gai, & Gottret, 2007).
- A higher reliance on OOP payments has been shown to contribute to worse health outcomes (United Nations Sustainable Development Solutions Network, 2015). For example, a 10% higher share of OOP payments was significantly associated with an average rise of 11.6 female deaths per 1000 (Moreno-Serra & Smith, 2011; United Nations Sustainable Development Solutions Network, 2015).
- In the United States, better adult and infant health outcomes have been clearly linked to the implementation and expansion of the Medicare and Medicaid schemes (Moreno-Serra & Smith, 2015).

- The introduction of the universal coverage scheme in Thailand has resulted in an estimated decrease of 6.5 infant deaths per 1000 births among the poor from 2001 to 2005 (Farahani, Subramanian, & Canning, 2010; Gruber, Hendren, & Townsend, 2013; Martin, Rice, & Smith, 2008).

Country case studies in high-income and middle-income settings provide further empirical evidence supporting UHC's positive impact on health (see Annex for further details on these and other country case studies). For example:

- Japan's mortality rates for communicable diseases in children and young adults started to decline and life expectancy at birth increased in the 1950s and early 1960s, when the government scaled up population health interventions and introduced universal health coverage (Ikeda et al., 2011).
- After the introduction of the Health Transformation Programme (HTP) in 2003, life expectancy in Turkey increased by 4 years between 2003 and 2013, half-a-year more rapidly than the average across OECD countries. Following an increased investment in the supply of primary care services, maternal and child health and infectious diseases improved significantly.
- Germany's social health insurance (SHI)—along with favourable socioeconomic factors—has contributed to an improvement in population health outcomes. Life expectancy at birth reached 81 years old in 2013, an increase of more than 10 years since 1960.

[...]

The Republican War Against Universal Health Care

Kenneth Peres

Kenneth Peres, retired, is the former Chief Economist for the Communications Workers of America.

After a short summer hiatus, the battle over health care policy reemerged with a passion last week when Senator Sanders introduced a version of "single payer" universal health care coverage and Senators Cassidy and Graham introduced yet another bill attempting to repeal Obamacare. These are just the latest eruptions of a longstanding war both for and against government supported comprehensive healthcare coverage and quality health care. It is an on-going war—a war that began with Teddy Roosevelt's 1912 presidential campaign and the Progressive Party, extended through the Roosevelt and Truman administrations, erupted with Medicare and Medicaid during the Johnson administration, faltered with HillaryCare during the Clinton administration, and exploded into the 21st century with the struggle over Obamacare.

This article will examine the Republican side of this war. Republicans hate government supported health care in general and Obamacare in particular for a number of reasons: ideological opposition to any major government program expenditures not directly benefitting big business and support for supposed "free" market policies that maintain private sector control and corporate domination; opposition to taxes on the wealthy and large corporations especially when those taxes are used to fund government programs that support moderate and low-income families including the Obamacare taxes that subsidize the cost of insurance to make it more affordable; a focus on limiting and

"The Republican War Against Government Supported Health Care," by Kenneth Peres, Common Dreams, September 22, 2017. https://www.commondreams.org/views/2017/09/22/republican-war-against-government-supported-health-care. Licensed under CC BY SA 3.0.

eliminating the availability of contraception and abortion; or a mix of all of these.

Given such opposition, Republicans have been engaged in a four-pronged attack against governmental programs that seek to improve the health of all Americans: introducing legislation to repeal and replace Obamacare; sabotaging and killing Obamacare through administrative fiat and court cases; significantly slashing funds for government health care programs; and eliminating environmental and workplace regulations and programs that protect people's health. There is a sense of urgency to complete this offensive because Republicans apparently want to register some kind of "win" in order to fulfill longstanding promises to gut Obamacare, roll back government supported health care programs and grant billions of dollars in tax cuts to large corporations and the wealthy—no matter the cost in human suffering.

The Legislative Attack on Government Supported Health Care

Not one of the Republican-sponsored bills to repeal/replace Obamacare included any plan to improve the health and welfare of most Americans. Not one of their bills sought to increase comprehensive coverage for the 28 million Americans who are still uninsured or to reduce premiums and out of pocket expenses for comprehensive coverage. Instead, every one of their proposed legislative bills would have led to the deaths of thousands of people and adverse impacts on the health of everyone—especially women, infants, and children. The only real beneficiaries of their health care schemes would be large corporations and wealthy individuals whose taxes would have been reduced.

Yet, these bills passed the House with the support of more than 90% of the Republican caucus and lost by just 1 vote in the Senate. Senators Cassidy and Graham introduced a new repeal bill last week proving that any of these bills can be resurrected at almost anytime subject to the legislative rules in each of the chambers. Here are just two examples to remind us of the disastrous consequences of these bills.

- The House and Senate repeal and/or replace bills would cause the deaths of an additional 170,000 to 294,000 Americans in the first ten years. The Congressional Budget Office estimated that the House health care bill would result in the loss of coverage for 23 million people. An analysis by the Center for American Progress estimated that the House bill would result in 217,000 additional deaths just over its first ten years relative to current law. Using the same methodology the so-called Skinny Repeal that was defeated in the Senate would have resulted in 16,000,000 people losing their insurance with an additional death toll of 170,000. The worst option proposed but defeated in the Senate would have been the repeal-only bill that would have resulted in 32,000,000 people losing coverage leading to 294,000 additional deaths over the first ten years. The CBO has not yet completed an analysis of the Cassidy-Graham bill; however, initial indications are that it is quite similar to the previous repeal-only bill.

- Waiving essential benefits would have especially undermined the health of millions of women and children. Obamacare requires all insurance plans to cover ten essential benefits including maternity insurance coverage for pregnancy, labor, delivery, and newborn baby care. Every one of the Republican House and Senate bills effectively allows states to waive these benefits. Nine million women gained maternity coverage after 2014 when Obamacare made it an essential benefit. Before then, only 12% of plans sold on the individual market included this coverage. Obamacare maternity coverage includes outpatient services such as prenatal and postnatal doctor visits, diabetes screenings, lab studies, medications, etc.; inpatient services such as hospitalization, doctor fees, etc.; newborn baby care; and lactation counseling and breast-pump rentals. This coverage also reduces maternal and infant mortality by improving the health of women before and during pregnancies and by preventing unintended pregnancies. Conversely, the lack of decent maternity coverage places the health of women and newborns at risk. The House and Senate bills also would adversely impact women and children by undermining other Obamacare essential benefits such as prescription drugs (women are more likely than men to need prescription drugs to meet their daily health care needs); lab tests such as Pap smears and mammograms; doctor visits (women account for 60% of outpatient visits); emergency room visits (women make 60% of emergency room visits); and hospitalization (women are 70% more likely than men to have had an inpatient hospital stay).

[…]

The Budgetary War Against Programs that Improve Health Care—Especially for Women, Infants and Children

While the media and public have focused attention on the attack against Obamacare, President Trump and House Republicans have also proposed budget plans that will cut trillions of dollars from health programs and basic assistance while promising massive tax cuts that will largely go to large corporations and the most wealthy members of our society. Children and women are among the groups that will be most harmed by these budget cuts. Here are some examples.

- Undermining the health of 49% of the children in the US. Thirty-six million children below 18 years of age are enrolled in Medicaid and the Children's Health Insurance Program (CHIP). This amounts to 49% of all children in the US. Ninety-five percent of children with Medicaid or CHIP coverage have a regular source of care compared to just 69% of children without coverage. Increased coverage means better health, lower mortality and decreased costs overall. Yet, President Trump and the House Republicans are targeting these children.

- Slashes $610 billion from Medicaid in addition to the $877 billion cut contained in the House health bill. This amounts to a total cut of $1.4 trillion or 47% over ten years. Medicaid cuts will adversely impact the health of pregnant women, newborns, infants and children. Medicaid pays for a significant portion of births in the US. The highest rate is New Mexico where Medicaid covers 72% of births while New Hampshire has the lowest rate of 27%. Half the states report that Medicaid covers more than 50% of births. Medicaid also is the single largest health insurer for children providing coverage for more than 30 million low-income children and children with disabilities. Dr. Steve Allen the CEO of Nationwide Children's Hospital in Columbus Ohio neatly sums up the issue: "Significant cuts to Medicaid will reduce access to health care for children who have it now, deny access or adequate care to children not yet born and lead to greater future medical costs by denying access to preventive care." Children with disabilities will be especially impacted. The Children's Hospital Association stated "The effects [of the budget cuts] on children are likely to be even more dramatic when considering those enrolled in Medicaid due to disability who have greater use of long-term care services and whose per enrollee costs are much higher than the traditional children group."

- Slashes the CHIP by 19% or $3.2 billion in just one year. The Trump budget only specifies one year of funding for CHIP—a program with approximately 6 million enrolled low-income children. This program covers well-child visits, immunizations, prescriptions, dental and vision care, in- and out-patient hospital care, X-rays, lab work and emergency services. Obviously, these services will be cut if Trump's budget is passed and millions of children will suffer.

- Denying food to 46 million needy people including 20 million children. The Trump budget proposes to cut $193 billion or

29% from the Supplemental Nutrition Assistance Program (food stamps) that feeds 46 million people including almost 20 million children. In 2012, this program helped keep 2.1 million children out of poverty. A Northwestern Institute for Policy Research brief states that "Mothers who receive food stamps while pregnant have a reduced risk of having a low-birth weight infant. Low birth weight is a major cause of infant mortality in the U.S."

- Making life more difficult for severely disabled children and their families. The Children's Defense Fund states that Trump's budget will slash $72 billion over ten years from the Supplemental Security Income Program (SSI), which covers more than 8 million children and adults with the most severe disabilities. SSI benefits are quite low—less than $650 per month for a disabled child. But these payments help the families of 1.2 million children meet the costs of child care or lost parental income due to caring for the child at home rather than an institution.

- Undermining the nutrition and health of women, infants and children. The Trump budget cuts $200 million from the Special Supplemental Nutrition Program for Women, Infants, and Children (WIC). But this may be just the opening salvo. In 2011, Republicans proposed a whopping 10% cut to WIC. WIC serves over 9 million mothers and young children, over 1.5 million pregnant and breastfeeding mothers, more than half of America's infants, and one-quarter of its children 1 to 5 years of age. WIC has been shown to improve birth outcomes and reduce risk factors for infant mortality—especially pre-term births. Preterm birth—babies born too soon and too small—is the leading overall cause of US infant mortality. The Institute of Medicine estimates that, in 2005, the annual societal economic cost associated with preterm birth was at least $26.2 billion in direct and indirect costs. The CIA World Fact Book for 2016 ranks the US as having the 57th lowest infant mortality rate—a rank much worse than almost all other developed countries and a number of developing countries. Even though we rank poorly, our infant mortality rate has been declining. This decline is due to more comprehensive health care and services especially for low-income women such as the neonatal care and maternal health and nutrition services provided through WIC. But this progress may be reversed with less coverage and fewer services.

- Eliminating the Teen Pregnancy Prevention Program. The Trump administration has ended the TPP program by slashing $214 million from its budget. The Centers for Disease Control reported that "in 2010, teen pregnancy and childbirth accounted for at least $9.4 billion in costs to U.S. taxpayers for increased health care and foster care, increased incarceration rates among children of teen parents, and lost tax revenue because of lower educational attainment and income among teen mothers." The TPP was a targeted program to prevent teen pregnancies especially in high-risk communities. This was accomplished by grants to various institutions around the country to conduct counseling, education and research. But in July the Center for Investigative Reporting broke the story that the administration "quietly axed" the remaining two years of the TPP grants. The TPP grants were supposed to serve approximately 1 million teenagers in high-risk communities over five years. This action is consistent with the House appropriations subcommittee plan to eliminate teen pregnancy prevention.

The Attack on Environmental and Workplace Programs and Regulations That Protect Everyone's Health

The administration and Congressional attack on any government program to support health quality is also taking place through the elimination or slashing of environmental and workplace programs and regulations. The attack on environmental programs is not only an attempt to assist corporate polluters and pad the profits of large corporations but also a means to make room for the coming massive tax breaks that will be proposed for large corporations and the wealthy. But guess who suffers from this dismantling of environmental programs and protections? Christine Todd Whitman, the EPA administrator under President W. Bush, even wrote an article for *The Atlantic* entitled "I ran George W. Bush's EPA and Trump's Cuts to the Agency Will Cost Lives." Here is a small sample of what is taking place and who will suffer.

- Giving more freedom to corporations to pollute while making taxpayers pay the costs and forcing workers and communities to suffer the health consequences. Funding for EPA will be cut by $2.6 billion or 31% with the loss of a quarter of the EPA workforce. The proposed budget cuts will significantly limit the EPA's ability to fulfill its purpose to "ensure that all Americans are protected from significant risks to human health and the environment where they live, learn and work." Especially hard hit will be programs that monitor air and water quality, enforce rules and regulations, penalize polluters, and clean up superfund sites and regional watersheds. The administration is thus cutting the ability of the EPA to protect people and hold corporations accountable for their actions. Corporations will be given much more freedom to pollute with impunity—they no longer will have to fear that the EPA has the ability to properly monitor pollution or impose penalties. Instead, the costs of pollution will be born by taxpayers and by the workers and communities that suffer from worse health.
- Approving dirtier air. Funding for the Clean Air Act will be cut by 50%. The budget cuts to the Clean Air Act are taking place despite evidence in favor of the economic and health benefits of the Act. According to the American Lung Association, nearly 40% of the US population lives in counties where they are "exposed to unhealthful levels of air pollution in the form of either ozone or short-term or year-round levels

of particles. Pregnant women and children are especially affected. For example, a Harvard University study released in 2013 concluded that pregnant women living in areas with elevated levels of air pollution 'were up to twice as likely' to have an autistic child compared with women in low-pollution locations." Furthermore, children living with air pollution are more likely to develop asthma.

• Sanctioning dirtier tap water and lead contamination. Grants to help states monitor the quality of public water systems will be cut by $31 million or 30%. In addition, the Trump budget would eliminate the Lead Risk Reduction Program, which spends $2.5 million every year to train workers to renovate buildings that contain lead paint and provide public education. Lead exposure can cause irreversible brain damage in children and disproportionately affects low-income families.

• Enabling dirtier sources of clean water. Funding for clean water in the Great Lakes Restoration Initiative (GLRI) will be cut by 90% from $300 million to just $10 million. The Great Lakes provides drinking water for 40 million residents of the US and Canada. Former EPA Administrator Whitman stated, "cutting the GLRI will result in significant increases in pollution and a return to some of the same problems that plagued this significant source of clean water for years to come. Surely in the wake of the Flint water crisis—where lead leached into the Michigan city's water supply after officials switched its source to the Flint River to cut costs—we can recognize this is not a risk worth taking." The Chesapeake Bay Program will also be eliminated leading to poorer water quality, unhealthy fish and seafood and the decimation of industries that depend on the Bay's seafood and water.

[…]

• Permitting the use of a pesticide known to damage children's brains. EPA Director Scott Pruitt took this action even though his own agency recommended that the pesticide, chlorpyrifos, be banned. An article in *Mother Jones* reported that "a number of studies found strong evidence that low doses of chlorpyrifos inhibits kids' brain development, including when exposure occurs in the womb, with effects ranging from lower IQ to higher rates of autism." The studies also found that "babies and fetuses are particularly susceptible to damage from chlorpyrifos because they metabolize toxic chemicals more slowly than adults do. And 'many adults' are susceptible, too, because they lack a gene that allows for metabolizing the chemical efficiently." Dow Chemical—the primary producer of the chemical—has actively fought against limiting the chemical's use and gave $1 million to Trump's inaugural committee.

- Ensuring that polluters DON'T pay. Federal Criminal and Civil Enforcement Cut by 40% and Enforcement Grants to States by 45%. The cuts will significantly curtail the ability of the federal enforcement office to ensure that corporations comply with federal regulations by monitoring polluters and imposing penalties. But the budget also cuts the grants that allow states to do that enforcement. The result will ensure that enforcement of environmental rules and regulations will be significantly reduced at both the federal and state levels.

[...]

So Far, the Republican Offensive Has Backfired

The Republicans have implemented a strategy to undermine Obamacare and destroy all vestiges of government support for comprehensive health coverage and health care quality. So far, this strategy has backfired. The Republican repeal/replace bills energized a significant, broad and active opposition by citizen groups and health care institutions and experts around the country. This opposition forced Democrats to hold the line and made it possible for at least three Republican Senators to vote against the Republican repeal/replace bills this past spring and summer. This was a narrow margin but a significant victory. Such mass activity will again be required to enable at least three Republican and all Democratic Senators to oppose the Cassidy-Graham repeal bill. This broad-based opposition will continue whether or not the Cassidy-Graham bill passes and could be an important factor in the 2018 and 2020 elections.

The Republican offensive also sought to forestall any efforts to "improve" Obamacare. However, it actually stimulated a number of Republicans and Democratic Senators to discuss reforms that might strengthen Obamacare. The Republicans leading this effort have pulled back during the fight over the Cassidy-Graham bill. Yet, such discussions may be revived if the latest repeal effort is defeated.

Finally, the Republican offensive was an attempt to deliver a generational deathblow to any proposals that would create a government-sponsored health care system requiring universal and comprehensive coverage. Yet, the Republican strategy apparently awakened a sleeping giant—a progressive movement to establish a truly universal health care system. It is now up to progressives to implement a strategy to achieve this goal.

Organizations to Contact

The editors have compiled the following list of organizations concerned with the issues debated in this book. The descriptions are derived from materials provided by the organizations. All have publications or information available for interested readers. This list was compiled on the date of publication of the present volume; the information provided here may change. Be aware that many organizations take several weeks or longer to respond to inquiries, so allow as much time as possible.

Centers for Medicare & Medicaid Services

7500 Security Blvd.
Baltimore, MD 21244-1850
phone: (800) 633-4227
website: www.medicare.gov/

The Centers for Medicare & Medicaid Services (CMS), a branch of the Department of Health and Human Services (HHS), is the federal agency that runs the Medicare Program. CMS also monitors Medicaid programs offered by each state. Medicare is funded through the Hospital Insurance Trust Fund and the Supplementary Medical Insurance Trust Fund.

The Commonwealth Fund

1 East 75th Street
New York, NY 10021
phone: (212) 606-3800
email: info@cmwf.org
website: www.commonwealthfund.org/

The Commonwealth Fund is a private foundation that aims to promote a high performing health care system that achieves better access, improved quality, and greater efficiency, particularly for society's most vulnerable members, including low-income individuals, the uninsured, minority Americans, young children, and the elderly.

The Cross Cultural Health Care Program
1200 12th Ave. S., Ste. 1001
Seattle, WA 98144-2712
phone: (206) 860-0329
email: administration@xculture.org
website: www.xculture.org/

The Cross Cultural Health Care Program (CCHCP) is a nonprofit training and consulting organization founded in 1992. Its mission is to serve as a bridge between communities and health care institutions to advance access to quality health care that is culturally and linguistically appropriate.

Kaiser Family Foundation
2400 Sand Hill Road
Menlo Park, CA 94025
phone: (650) 854-9400
email: kaiserfamilyfoundationsubscriptions@kff.org
website: www.kff.org/

A leader in health policy analysis and health journalism, the Kaiser Family Foundation is dedicated to filling the need for trusted information on national health issues. Kaiser is a nonprofit organization focused on national health issues, as well as the role of the US in global health policy. Kaiser develops and runs its own policy analysis, journalism, and communications programs.

National Institutes of Health
9000 Rockville Pike
Bethesda, Maryland 20892
phone: (301) 496-4000
email: NIHinfo@od.nih.gov
website: www.nih.gov/

The National Institutes of Health (NIH), a part of the US Department of Health and Human Services, is the nation's medical research agency. It focuses on making important discoveries that improve health and save lives.

Planned Parenthood Federation of America
123 William Street, 10th Floor
New York, NY 10038
phone: (800) 430-4907
website: www.plannedparenthood.org/

Planned Parenthood is one of the nation's leading providers of high-quality, affordable health care for women, men, and young people and the nation's largest provider of sex education. It offers quality health care backed by medical experts and over 100 years of research in reproductive care.

US Department of Health & Human Services (HHS)
200 Independence Avenue, SW
Washington, DC 20201
phone: (877) 696-6775
website: www.hhs.gov

It is the mission of the US Department of Health & Human Services (HHS) to enhance and protect the health and well-being of all Americans. They fulfill that mission by providing effective health and human services and fostering advances in medicine, public health, and social services.

World Health Organization (WHO)
525 23rd Street, NW
Washington, DC 20037
phone: (202) 974-3000
website: www.who.int/en/

The World Health Organization's goal is to build a better, healthier future for people all over the world. Working through offices in more than 150 countries, WHO staff work side by side with governments and other partners to ensure the highest attainable level of health for all people.

Bibliography

Books

Donald A. Barr. *Introduction to US Health Policy: The Organization, Financing, and Delivery of Health Care in America*. Baltimore, MD: John Hopkins University Press, 2016.

Patricia Boling. *The Politics of Work–Family Policies: Comparing Japan, France, Germany and the United States*. New York, NY: Cambridge University Press, 2015.

Elizabeth H. Bradley and Lauren A. Taylor. *The American Health Care Paradox: Why Spending More Is Getting Us Less*. New York, NY: Public Affairs, 2013.

David Goldhill. *Catastrophic Care: Why Everything We Think We Know About Health Care Is Wrong*. New York, NY: Knopf Doubleday Publishing Group, 2013.

Tara Haelle. *Vaccination Investigation: The History and Science of Vaccines*. Minneapolis, MN: Twenty-First Century Books, 2018.

Douglas E. Hough. *Irrationality in Health Care: What Behavioral Economics Reveals About What We Do and Why*. Palo Alto, CA: Stanford University Press, 2013.

Lawrence R. Jacobs and Theda Skocpol. *Health Care Reform and American Politics: What Everyone Needs to Know*. New York, NY: Oxford University Press, 2016.

Mike King. *A Spirit of Charity: Restoring the Bond Between America and Its Public Hospitals*. Salisbury, MD: Secant Publishing LLC, 2016.

Edward D. Kleinbard. *We Are Better Than This: How Government Should Spend Our Money*. New York, NY: Oxford University Press, 2014.

Chris Kresser. *Unconventional Medicine: Join the Revolution to Reinvent Healthcare, Reverse Chronic Disease, and Create a Practice You Love*. Austin, TX: Lioncrest Publishing, 2017.

Roman Krznaric. *Empathy: Why It Matters, and How to Get It*. New York, NY: Penguin, 2014.

Elisabeth Rosenthal. *An American Sickness: How Healthcare Became Big Business and How You Can Take It Back*. New York, NY: Penguin, 2017.

Prabhjot Singh. *Dying and Living in the Neighborhood: A Street-Level View of America's Healthcare Promise.* Baltimore, MD: John Hopkins University Press, 2016.

Rachel E. Spector. *Cultural Diversity in Health and Illness.* New York, NY: Pearson Education, 2016.

Paul Starr. *The Social Transformation of American Medicine: The Rise of a Sovereign Profession and the Making of a Vast Industry.* New York, NY: Basic Books, 2017.

H. Gilbert Welch. *Overdiagnosed: Making People Sick in the Pursuit of Health.* Boston, MA: Beacon Press, 2011.

Jonathan Wolff. *The Human Right to Health.* New York, NY: W. W. Norton & Company, 2012.

Periodicals and Internet Sources

Steven Anderson. "A brief history of Medicare in America Landmark social program now covers 49.4 million Americans." *Medicare Resources,* October 27, 2016. https://www.medicareresources.org/basic-medicare-information/brief-history-of-medicare/.

Tyler Cowen. "Poor U.S. Scores in Health Care Don't Measure Nobels and Innovation," *New York Times,* October 5, 2006. http://www.nytimes.com/2006/10/05/business/05scene.html.

Ross Douthat. "Make America Singapore." *New York Times,* March 18, 2017. https://www.nytimes.com/2017/03/18/opinion/sunday/make-america-singapore.html.

Randi Druzin. "Frustrated by long waits, some Canadians are heading to U.S. for medical treatment." *US News,* August 3, 2016. https://www.usnews.com/news/best-countries/articles/2016-08-03/canadians-increasingly-come-to-us-for-health-care.

Benjamin Y. Fong and Dustin Guastella. "America Needs A Healthcare System Built For Care, Not Profit." *Huffington Post,* January 17, 2018. https://www.huffingtonpost.com/entry/united-states-healthcare-medicare-for-all-bernie-sanders_us_5a5f397ee4b096ecfca908cc.

Jon Greenberg. "Bernie Sanders: U.S. 'only major country' that doesn't guarantee right to health care." *Politifact,* June 29, 2015. http://www.politifact.com/truth-o-meter/statements/2015/jun/29/bernie-s/bernie-sanders-us-only-major-country-doesnt-guaran/.

David Kelley. "Is There a Right to Health Care?" *Atlas Society*, May 12, 2010. https://atlassociety.org/commentary/understanding-obamacare/obamacare-blog/3652-is-there-a-right-to-health-care.

Danielle Kurtzleben. "Study: Sanders' Proposals Would Add $18 Trillion To Debt Over 10 Years." *NPR*, May 9, 2016. https://www.npr.org/2016/05/09/477402982/study-sanders-proposals-would-add-18-trillion-to-debt-over-10-years.

Michael F. Mulroy, "Universal health care is an economic necessity." *Seattle Times*, January 5, 2018. https://www.seattletimes.com/opinion/universal-health-care-is-an-economic-necessity/.

Vann R. Newkirk II. "A Political Opening for Universal Health Care?" *Atlantic*, February 14, 2017. https://www.theatlantic.com/politics/archive/2017/02/universal-health-care-polls-obamacare-repeal/516504/.

Noam Scheiber. "How Obamacare Actually Paves the Way Toward Single Payer." *New Republic*, January 5, 2014. https://newrepublic.com/article/116105/obamacare-will-lead-single-payer-michael-moore.

Jacque Wilson. "Your health care is covered, but who's going to treat you?" *CNN*, June 29, 2012. http://www.cnn.com/2012/06/29/health/doctor-shortage-affordable-care-act/index.html.

Index

A

accountable care organizations (ACOs), 53, 116–121
Affordable Care Act (ACA)/ ObamaCare, 18, 27–29, 31, 33, 34, 36, 47, 65, 67, 69, 94, 96, 116, 117, 129, 131, 148, 157–167
Agence France-Presse (AFP), 129–131
Algorithms for Innovation, 122–128
Almeida, Jose, 36–38
American Health Care Act (AHCA), 25, 27–29, 33, 34, 35
Anderson, Chloe, 47–56

B

bankruptcy, medical debt as number one reason for, 15, 34
Bartolone, Pauline, 65–68
Bialik, Kristen, 94–96
Booker, Cory, 33
Boudreau, Richard, 18–24

C

California proposal for single-payer system, 65–68, 70

Canada, health care system in, 23, 24, 47, 49, 50, 51, 70, 92, 93, 148–152
Chalkidou, Kalipso, 139–147
Cho, Joshua, 33–35
Chua, Kao-Ping, 73–80
Clinton, Bill, 58, 130, 157
Clinton, Hillary, 130, 131, 157

D

diabetes, 52, 82, 86–89, 127, 159
Dolan, Ed, 25–29
Durand-Zaleski, Isabelle, 97–105

E

employer-sponsored insurance, 14, 26, 27, 28, 49, 60, 65, 66, 68, 70, 71, 73, 74, 75, 78, 79, 98–99, 130

F

France, health care system in, 30, 47, 48, 49, 51, 97–105, 130

G

Germany, health care system in, 22, 23, 47, 51, 78, 130, 156

Gold, Jenny, 116–121
government spending, smarter,
    how to ensure, 86–89

H

health care, US
  as federal responsibility, 15,
    91–93, 94–96
  as a privilege and not a right,
    16, 129–131
health care system, US
  comparison to other
    nations, 14, 29, 47–56
  overview and state of,
    18–24, 25–29, 30–32,
    108–109
  reasons for rising costs, 81–85
Hogberg, David, 57–64

I

insurance, private, 14, 15, 26,
    27, 28, 29, 35, 41, 44, 49,
    58–59, 60, 61, 62, 66, 67,
    70, 74, 75, 81, 82, 85, 95,
    98–99, 119, 130, 144, 149,
    150, 151

J

Japan, health care system in,
    47, 49, 50, 78, 156
Johnson, Jake, 30–32

K

Kennedy, Edward, 59, 60, 61
Konduri, Niranjan, 86–89
Kuttner, Robert, 81–85

L

Lavidge, Kathleen A., 106–109

M

Malcolm, Candice, 148–152
Medicaid, 14, 26, 31, 32, 43, 44,
    49, 67, 70, 73–74, 79, 95,
    130, 155, 157, 160, 161
Medicare, 14, 26, 30, 34, 39,
    40, 41–42, 43, 44, 49,
    57–64, 66, 69–72, 76,
    81, 92, 95, 107, 116, 117,
    118–119, 130, 155, 157
"Medicare for All" proposal,
    30, 34, 57–64, 66, 69–72
Moffit, Robert E., 69–72

O

Obama, Barack, 34, 44, 69,
    118, 129, 131
Office of the United Nations
    High Commissioner for
    Human Rights, 110–115
Organisation for Economic
    Co-operation and
    Development (OECD),
    153–156

P

Peres, Kenneth, 157–167

R

Roosevelt, Franklin, 129, 157
Rovner, Julie, 91–93

S

Sanders, Bernie, 34, 69–72,
    131, 157
Smith, Dennis, 39–45
Smith, Peter C., 139–147
Squires, David, 30, 47–56
Sustainable Development
    Solutions Network
    (SDSN), 133–138

T

Truman, Harry, 129, 157
Trump, Donald, 33, 96, 129, 148,
    160, 161, 162, 163, 165, 166

U

UK, health care system in, 22,
    23, 24, 31, 48, 49, 50, 51, 52,
    70, 85, 87, 106–107, 109,
    126–127, 130, 144, 145, 146
universal health care
  arguments against, 16, 18,
      39–45
  arguments for, 73–80,
      106–109

and better health, 153–156
California proposal for
    single–payer system,
    65–68, 70
cost of, 74–75
as human right, 15, 18, 35,
    110, 111, 114, 115, 134,
    150
political support/lack of
    support for, 33–35,
    157–167
public support for, 94–96
Republican war against, 30,
    32, 129, 157–167
unnecessary treatments,
    36–38, 82, 117, 123

V

Veterans Administration, 26

W

Warren, Elizabeth, 72
Wasserman-Schultz, Debbie,
    34–35
World Health Organization
    (WHO), 30, 86, 87, 88,
    136, 139